ANCHOR BOOKS

PERCEPTIONS

First published in Great Britain in 1994 by
ANCHOR BOOKS
1-2 Wainman Road, Woodston,
Peterborough, PE2 7BU

Foreword

Anchor Books is a small press, established in 1992, with the aim of promoting readable poetry to as wide an audience as possible.

We hope to establish an outlet for writers of poetry who may have struggled to see their work in print.

Following our request in the National Press, we were overwhelmed by the response. The poems presented here have been selected from many entries. Editing proved to be a difficult and daunting task and as the Editor, the final selection was mine.

The poems chosen represent a cross-section of styles and content. They have been sent from all over the country, written by young and old alike, united in the passion for writing poetry.

I trust this selection will delight and please the authors and all those who enjoy reading poetry.

Michelle Abbott
Editor

Contents

Freedom
Around the country I have roamed,
No place to call my home,
From town to town, I've ambled round,
But a home, I never found.

The cold has bit my fingers,
As I've stood outside shop windows,
Watching the world pass me by,
No one sees me, for me they do not cry.

Now the snow begins to fall,
To my youth my mind recalls,
A life of comfort, I once had,
A happy healthy little lad.

Many times I think of my family,
I wonder, do they also think of me
But it was I who chose this life,
No commitments, no family, no wife.

So I amble from street to street,
A poor old chap, with tired old feet,
But save your pity, it's not for me,
Remember it was I, who chose to be free.
P Skipworth

Wish
The air clings around the body
Pressing slowly into my brain
Indenting my eyes as the candle
Flickers nervously once again.

An owl is howling at the night
As the song treads over my ear
Another thought, another sigh
And I still wish that you were here.
Laura Maynard

Thoughts of Thomas

I think of you as the winter winds blow and the earth is covered
in ice and snow
Why did you leave me? I do not know but it was God's will
that you should go,
I think of you now spring is here it is very hard for me to bear
I think of you but you are not there.
I think of you in the autumn glow, when the summer sun has gone
I think of you in the ice and snow as the winter gales blow strong,
I think of you that spring is here and the flowers are all blooming
I think of you in the still of night when all the world is sleeping
I think of you in your resting place where God His watch is keeping.
I think of you at the dawn of day, when bird songs fill the air
When the cuckoo sings and the sun breaks through
I think of you but you are not there,
The flowers you planted are everywhere, telling me of your love
But now you are in God's garden resting above.
For his love will surround you, and you are at peace
You left me oh so suddenly there was so much to say
But my dear one you are only a thought away,
I think of you as I walk alone along the country lanes
Through fields and woods and meadow rough where we
so loved to roam,
I think of you when the moon is high shining in a cloudless sky
And how I wish that you were here, and I was not alone.
I think of you on a summer day, when the grass is green
where the cricketers play
Where you loved to be in God's fresh air. I think of
you but you are not there.
I think of you and know my love
That you are in God's care above. I think of you in
your favourite chair,
I think and look but you are not there,

2

I think of you when I see our sons. Their wives and children too
I think oh what a legacy I have been left by you,
I think of you as I kneel in prayer
I think of you in God's care
And I know that you are there.
Alison G Briggs

Only to Me

It doesn't matter, you can't make it tonight,
You're miles away but it's quite alright,
Out of sight is out of mind they say, and yet
I find you're everywhere, in front of me.
Wherever I turn, I never learn to close my eyes
to let it go, don't overreact, don't make a scene,
I know you didn't mean to open the door, and
offer me more, then slam it unknowingly in my face,
and unwittingly fall from grace in my eyes. But
it's no surprise. I should have known, should have
stayed alone. But I'll try again, it doesn't
matter if I fall on my face, I'll get up again,
try and regain my cool, and risk looking a fool.
I'll do my best to understand. I won't expect
and I won't demand. I doesn't matter, it's not a
crime, you call the tune and I'll dance in time.
If I can and I must, and I'll learn to trust in
you in time. It doesn't matter, it's no big deal.
It's just how I feel when you can't be here, even
though you call, it really doesn't matter at all.
I'll be hurt but you won't know, I might be mad
but I won't let it show.

I'll look for a sign, and wait for a touch.
I won't let on that I care too much.
It doesn't matter at all you see.
It doesn't matter,
                    only to me.
Teresa Kerin

3

Where No Shadows Fall

Bleak, remote islands, battered
by winds and squall,
There lie our fallen heroes
who answered to the call.
They did not ask or reason why
When they sailed across the sea,
They only knew it was their task
to set those islands free.
But now they rest on hallowed ground,
this was their final call.
Rest in peace oh brave young men
where no shadows fall.
People of the islands, let no one
'ere forget
the price they paid for freedom
and how that price was met.
Lie down oh weary soldiers,
valiant warriors, brave young men.
Lay down your arms, the war is won,
the isles are free again.
Weep not the women of the dead,
for your tears cannot recall,
Let your loved ones rest in peace,
where no shadows fall.

A tribute to those who were left behind.
Frank Aulton

The Reason Why

Once upon a time, one sunny day,
I visited a land where black sheep were at play,
They sprang around all day and knew not why,
Trying with all their might to reach the sky.
The land was filled with the tallest trees
Growing in rows of fours and threes.

4

My friends and I sat against a wall
And watched the sheep rise and fall.
One by one they jumped up so high,
Looking as though they wanted to fly.
Soon they sprang higher than the tallest trees
Their ears pinned back by the breeze.
Sadly they knew not how to land . . .
And came crashing down into the sand.
But they had reached their goals
And were quite happy to die
And that, my friend, is the reason why.
Paulina Rusyn

Fear
Bleaching my mind of all I know, so confused, can't think straight.
Gripped by the sudden realisation that I am alone. I'm frightened!
Do I move? If so which way? Left, right, forwards or back
The overwhelming silence, broken only by a piercing scream.
Or is it? I'm convinced it's my imagination, working over time!
Pitch-black! The darkness encases me, consuming, devouring me.
Fear! All I know is fear, fear overpowering my common sense.
The only presence in this darkness is myself, so why am I nervous?
My heart is racing! Pumping adrenalin around every vein in my body.
Commanding myself to relax, with every breath I suffer complete
                                                    numbness.
Terrifying visions crowd my mind, filling the void like a landslide
                                                    into a chasm
Calm down! Must try to bring myself within the bounds of
                                                    rationalisation.
Why place myself in this predicament?
I repeatedly ask myself pausing a moment, I deeply inhale
Then retort my answer while exhaling. To overcome!
To conquer and master this phobia, so order prevails.
Why am I paranoid in the dark?
I suppose I fear the unseen, the unknown.

Constantly reminding myself of my objective, to confront this
                              emptiness heartbeat slows down,
I'm succeeding fear's losing its grip! Now I know I have won!
Also I enhance my self-belief.
For I have confronted this once crippling, once limiting state of mind!
Feeling complete. In the knowledge I have just strengthened
                                        my character.
For once I am thinking positively, for I have made the transition.
No longer a boy, now I am a man!
S McCoy

The Prisoner

They will come as darkness peels
Back from where my scarred frame kneels,
Through broken lips I curse each dawn
My respite from their torture gone.

Can I yet more beatings take
Are there yet more limbs to break,
Or shall my voice in pain exude
That which will my life conclude.

I chill as in the darkness clear
The short shrill cry of rats draws near,
Through fear I scream and beat around
Yet watching cruel, small eyes abound.

Tears well up in sunken eyes
Yet courage courses and defies,
Self pity which would weakness show
My will to break at daylight's glow.

I start to retch and panic grows
For peering 'round the dawning shows,
Oh would I that in life beyond
The torturers were tortured ones.

Shall I failing strength unite
To claw the fence which bars my flight,
Yet other souls have tried in vain
It haunts me yet their cries of pain.

Yes they will come but soon too late
For death desires her greed to sate,
My lips sealed still yet no more pain
My spirit free to roam again.
J B Yates

Beggars

When walking the streets you're bound to find
A beggar,
Asking you to be kind,
To spare a few pennies, or even a pound maybe,
So he can buy some food
To fill him sufficiently.
But when you see that beggar, sitting on the ground,
You'll be scared by his appearance,
You'll be scared by his frown,
You'll think he's a lowlife with no future interest
But to spend his life on the streets
Being a pest.
And when you walk past him, you'll never see what he bears
The fear, the anguish,
And the shame that he wears,
To be humiliated in the streets, begging, to keep alive,
When he knows very well
What people are thinking inside.
So while you're walking past with an air of disgrace,
You'll probably never get to see
The look upon his face

The look, that for life, will bear a big stain,
The look that if you cared enough
Will show you his pain,
The look that would separate a sufferer from a con
The look that would tell you
That all hope is gone.
Natasha Teeluck

Top Hat and Tales
I used to be so happy,
But now I'm full of regret,
For the magic went out of our marriage,
When the wife sold my conjuring set.

I didn't mind her ripping up the cards,
Or burning my favourite silk scarf,
It was when she picked up the black and decker,
And sawed my assistant in half.

I got the blame for the bloodshed,
I was the one in the cell,
She even took away my white rabbits,
And sold them to Dewhurst's as well.

I just wish she had been satisfied,
Instead of reading those sex manuals,
I mean, I'm not that bad a lover,
And I've got much more hair than Paul Daniels.

She took away all of our savings,
And left me to starve, cold and poor,
Then she ran away with the circus,
I just can't perform anymore.

So all I've got left is my top hat,
A bow tie and one single white glove,
I wish I had someone to talk to,
But I've just eaten my last turtle dove.

Now I sleep under railway arches,
On park benches and in muddy ditches,
While she's ran off with a tattooed man,
So every night she's up the pictures.
Ed Vickers

Time

You gave me time to get myself into a relaxed, carefree state,
You always said, 'Take your time, don't hurry, other things can wait,'
I'm glad for all the hours, we spent, talking always being fair,
Perhaps that's why I miss you, so much when you're not there.

Time heals so many people say but how long does hurt last,
Two people loving, sharing, living their lives, now looking to the past,
For who knows what disaster may occur, to change the
course for two,
Now it's time to carry on, the me, without the You.
Karen Cooper

Disenchanted

Could I but find a place in which to dwell,
Where solitude and respite could find,
Then pen to paper I could put, and tell,
Of all the things in life I've left behind.

But places such as this are rare today,
For life is one big pantomime -
Oh how I'd like to get away,
Another place, another scene, another time.

For age is creeping up, I'm truly past my best,
And no one really cares a tinker's cuss,
So I'd like to get away and take a rest -
From all the ballyhoo and all the fuss.

When you're young, you crave for lots and lots of money,
To bring you happiness when you are very old,
But no matter what success you have, it's funny,
You never seem to find that crock of gold.

So you stagger to the edge of life's fulfilment,
Feeling shattered, disillusioned and unknown,
And you wonder where all the good ambitions went -
And why you're broke, and very much alone.

So here's the moral of this story,
Take all that's going when you're very, very young,
For late in life it's never hunk-e-dory,
The plans you had have somehow all gone wrong.

In consolation you will think of all the good days,
Pretend the bad days had never really been.
And you'll console yourself that in some ways,
All is well, and what has been, has been.
Thomas Parry

Baby Blues

Aunt Julie's baby's just learnt to crawl.
He just won't sit still at all!
They came to see us last weekend
It nearly drove me round the bend!

'You're not allowed the rubbish bin!
Look! It's got all the rubbish in!'
'Don't eat that! It isn't clean!
Ugh! You don't know where it's been!'

'Don't cry! Look, have this instead!'
'Watch out! He's going to bang his head!'
'Who left that there? He's hurt himself!
Ben! Fetch the cream on the kitchen shelf!'

'There, there! Don't cry! Poor little mite!
You're not hurt really. Just a fright.'
'Ben! Don't just sit there! Find a toy!
Keep him amused now, there's a good boy.'

I got my brand new laser gun
And blew his brains out, just for fun.
He didn't really seem to mind
But Mum said 'Stop it Ben! Be kind!'

I was done in when they finally went.
My toys were soggy. My books were bent.
Then something struck me! I wonder! Maybe . . .
It will stop Mum wanting another baby!
Gill Phillips

I Knew I'd Miss That Bus

I knew I'd miss that bus
From the moment I awoke and cursed the alarm clock,
Even before I burnt the toast
And spilled the sugar
I knew I'd miss that bus.
About the same time I realised all the milk was gone
Poured gaily onto cornflakes, being eaten by the children
Shouting between mouthfuls
I can't find my maths book
I knew I'd miss that bus.

Becoming absolute certainty during a game of hide and seek
                                              with my front door key
And turning my purse inside out to find the right change
And yet
If I run
Run faster
I knew I'd miss that bus.
Janet Butler

Keith Mentor and Friend

I was violent and vibrant, not much in control,
Of my life or my work with no thought for my soul.

You brought to my life, a way gentle, with silence.
You showed me the path from turmoil and violence.

You taught me. You helped me. You gave nothing but kindness.
I'm so sorry I repaid you with teenage blindness.

For thirty years and more, I've hoped I'd meet you again,
Just to say thank you, for the release from pain.

When I first knew you, I was fifteen years old,
In the world on my own feeling bitter and cold.

I'd found a place to live, got myself out of school.
Dodged the fist of my father, got from under his rule.

Not much in my father was decent or kind.
Get drunk. Thump the family. Was his way to unwind.

So I got out. Thinking out would be better:
I soon learned that *out* was even colder and wetter.

I so often wished I could have chosen a Dad,
That I couldn't chose you, was a regret I long had.

Those women we worked with gave me a surprise,
Their spite and cruelty really opened my eyes.

So I became clever and like them, hard.
To survive in that place I need that guard.

Then I met you. So gentle, so caring,
You turned me right round and put back the sharing.

I married the lad I was going to *throw*,
'Cause he wasn't clever with a lot of show.

My marriage lasts even now.
I thank you friend for showing me how.
To be gentle and caring and still be strong
And when to admit that I am wrong.
Pat Rice

This Country

This country is turning round,
Turning away with frustration;
Everything has to start anew
'What you doing about it?'

Take a step back and look what's happening around you.
This country has got to change
'What you doing about it?'

There are too many people,
Jobless, sick and hungry;
In this Godforsaken country,
'What you doing about it?'

Too much censorship and it cuts to the bone,
What is the meaning of a free country?
Does it mean free speech, this is a Calcutt Free Zone
If you really want a free country,
'What you doing about it?'

Too many conmen working for the system pushing pens,
Too much censorship for the camera lens,
Too many problems for a country to survive
'What you doing about it?'

Got to set this country's best minds to overdrive,
Cos this is what will make this country survive;
If you think negative, you can't be productive,
'So what you doing about it?'
Thomas J Kane

A Genuine Man

I see you slipping away
Further from reach
My hand, fingers outstretched
To hold you back
But I have no right.

Breathe breathe breathe
Let your judgement prevail.
Don't leave me stranded
Don't leave me.

Blood blood blood
It's not as thick as
You may think,
It seems the pen is mightier
Than that too.

I tried to see the world
Through mix's squinted eyes,
But the salt veil still falls

Real men don't go to pieces

14

I can't stop you, but
I won't help you!
I still remember the hair ribbons
And Billy was mine.

So I'll sit alone at the top of the
world, and search for
the book
To prove it wasn't a judgement.

Not enough too late.
I P Atheos

Little Angel
February 11th 1993, I felt such joy and wonder,
Come from within me,
As I looked down from my hospital bed,
'Congratulations it's a baby girl.'
The nurse said.

The following day, though
I did not know,
Another Mother's bundle of joy
Had been taken in such sorrow.

When released in the papers
And on the TV
Such a sad feeling came over
me, the tears fell from
My eyes and the pain hurt
Deep in my heart.
How could this have happened
To a lovely looking lad.
The Lord gives and the Lord
Taketh away,
So that is what the Bible says.

But what happened to Jamie
was not God's way
'Suffer the little children
that cometh to me.'
At least now he's safe,
And happy, no more hurt
for Jamie will there be.

He had the face of an angel
And deserves to be,
I never knew you little angel
or your family,
But when I look at my
children, I think of thee.

As one mother to another,
It really hurts me,
For Jamie really was a
beautiful baby.
But I hope life brings
back happiness with your
new child when born.

Though Jamie you will never
be forgotton,
Even by strangers like me.
For you are the little angel
Who lives on in all
Good children be.

Jamie you are special,
To all your family,
Just like all my children
Are special to me.

Although I never knew you,
You lived in a different city
There's a special place
In my heart
For you, little Jamie.
Annette Robbins

Kristopher Thirteen and a Half Months
Our little boy now can walk
A few little words he will also talk
He giggles with glee when his Daddy he espies
Who is the greatest fun in Kristopher's eyes,
Mummy is there for when he's tired and sleepy
To cuddle up to when he's feeling weepy
I could hardly believe my eyes
When he fed himself to my surprise!
He only has two little teeth with which to bite
But that in no way diminishes his appetite
He gobbles his food with sheer delight
'Til there's not a crumb or a morsel in sight,
His Daddy did the same thing too
So really that is nothing new
Clothes on radiators he does abhor
He takes them off and wipes the floor.
A little paddy he sometimes displays
But it's soon forgotten with his charming ways
A chatterbox he'll probably be
And I'll read him stories at my knee,
Brighten our lives? no doubt about that
Now we look forward to his *baby chat*.
Kristopher's Grandmother.
Jennifer Morbey Myatt

Fact or Fantasy

Where do kids of ten in England, learn to kill and maim,
From video's they should not watch and parents are to blame.
I've been in homes of people, very late at night,
I've seen these films and I don't think they are a pretty sight.
Sitting there besides you kids of nine or ten,
Watching films of violence, and the slaughter of fellow men.
It hardens them to gruesome sights and scenes they should not see,
Films so sick in nature they sicken adults like me.
Young kids today they watch them, brainwashed by it all,
Just as we were years ago as I can just recall.
We came out of the cinema, our heroes imitate,
Pretending to kill off indians that we'd been taught to hate.
Aliens and animals fell before my gun,
Nothing that I found in my way was safe beneath the sun.
I know we did not really kill but I wonder if I would,
If I was sniffing aerosols and I went out for blood.
Imagine you're a child of ten and the big kids showed you how,
To sniff the glue and get you high. I wonder could you now.
Your heads awash from solvent abuse and violence
                                                            enters your mind,
You just might kill in that atmosphere, I'm pretty sure you'll find.
So let us teach our children the right things from the start
Remove the hatred from the mind put love back in the heart.
Send kids to bed an early hour. Dad's be boss again.
Don't let the next kid in the dock bring you heartache and pain.
Geoffrey Alan Chapman

Reflections

I've never seen bright northern lights,
or stars shine on the Milky Way.
But I've seen a cool clear waterfall
framed by the blossoms of scented May.

I've walked in fields of sky blue flax
picked wild cherries on carefree days.
Paddled in stony Bourne Brook stream,
warmed by the sun's bright golden rays.

18

I've never seen the Eiffel Tower
or gazed at Niagara falls.
But I've watched the golden sunset
heard sonorous, wild Vixen calls.

I've walked a wood by soft moonlight.
Picked Blackberries in field and lane.
Built snowmen and a secret Den,
seen frost upon a window pane.

I've watched snowflakes falling lightly,
to make a white, crisp, Fairyland.
I've seen cobwebs on the Hawthorn,
touched by a secret, magic hand.

I may not see the Pyramids or travel
far flung, foreign climes.
But my mind has stored the riches
of all the good fulfilling times.
Sheila Swinnerton

Companions
Who knows where his life started
Your own special friend
He's loyal and devoted
Hours with you he'll spend.

You now have each other
to care for and caress
Someone to cook a meal for
and clear up all his mess!!

I wonder if he will change his scent
and roll around in the dirt
He may have an eye for the ladies
He may be quite a flirt!

So long as he doesn't lift his leg
upon the three piece suite
Else he'll find a toe shoved up his bum,
Then be denied of all his treats!

Though knowing you it won't be long
We know he's won your heart
The two of you walk side by side
A new life - new hope - a new start.
Lin Ellis

Cars and People

The cars speed along, some are good some are bad.
Along the roads they speed, the driver cares for no one.
Around the bend, around the corner along the play street,
                                    he speeds along.
Does he or she but mainly he care for young or old, on foot
                                    or bike, does he realise,
People are getting older, that they cannot go down subways,
or over bridges, but must cross the level road because
their knees or legs cannot climb or bend.
Do they slow down or anticipate that someone young or old may be
so scared to slow down or even stop;
To let someone cross even if they are too slow
For the pelican and get left stranded in the middle of the road only a
few more seconds or perhaps a minute just to give way, why
so pompous, why so impatient, why the horn pipping and howling
and shouting to see someone getting across our busy roads safely.
So drivers beware of young and old or perhaps
someone with their mind on something else, forgetting
for a split second or two, just to look left and right, it could be you.
Be patient anticipate all types of roads because
in these days and times anything could pop up or happen,
from cat to dog, from birds to fly, from holes in the road,
to gas mains, water or electricity cables, from grease or mud,
fog or rain but remember black ice, leaves and snow.

20

Remember too, people are getting older and slower look out
for the pram and pushchair between the cars children and
animals being pushed out first.
Remember pubs are open all day, so you must be on guard all the
time, look out for the bike and the motor bike, give them plenty
of room day and night.
Look for the bike without any lights it's too late when you hit him.
So drive carefully leave your aggression behind and be polite.
M R Sooklall

Coma

I stood at the gates, but they would not let me in.
And yet I thought I had done no great sin.
I watched the others as they passed me by,
And still I kept thinking and wondering why.
Then I heard a voice saying, 'Go back my son,
Your work on earth is not yet done.
When it is I will send for you,
Then you will find they will let you through.'
As I slowly opened my eyes and looked around,
I heard someone say he's coming 'round.
I saw my loved ones with tears in their eyes,
I knew they had been saying their last goodbyes.
I said I am getting better, can't you see?
They are not ready yet for me.
Now I know when my life's end is near,
For to leave this world and those I love dear.
To reach eternity, with stories untold,
To where the mysteries of life and death must unfold.
Henry Wardingley

Untitled

Civilisation! The Saviour of man
With the throwaway bottle. The throwaway can
Polystyrene block, for miracle packs
Throw your throwaway rubbish, into throwaway sacks
Useless junk mail, in flash plastic jackets
Throw away cartons, and throwaway packets
Civilisation! A plastic charade.
'Get your throwaway money' with your new plastic card
The devil will laugh at this *throwaway joke*
And watch with contempt as we all slowly choke
Drowned in the rubbish of a throw away tide
With nowhere to run. Nowhere to hide
From this man made Hell, we so proudly display
Civilisation! We threw it away.
Ron Ellis

The Council House Doors

'We've got four shades,' the painter said.
'Green or yellow, blue or red.
Just take your pick the choice is yours
What colour would you like your doors?'
'Oh! Yellow's nice,' I gaily cried.
But the painter shook his head and sighed.
'Yellow, he said, if laid on thick,
As it has to be, looks just like sick.'
'Alright then, green! That's not too bad.'
But the painter coughed and looked quite sad.
'Green,' he said. We haven't got -
Next door emptied the very last pot.'
'Never mind,' I consoled him. Let's settle for blue.'
But again, he sighed. 'Oh that won't suit you
For it's so pale within a day.
It fades to a miserable dirty grey.'
'So,' I moaned 'Then make it red.'
'Well it's up to you.' The painter said.
E A Groves

Our World
I used to walk amongst the flowers,
Spending many happy hours.
Birds in plenty used to sing,
Especially so to herald spring.
But now with trees and bushes spare,
Nesting and breeding are getting rare.
I used to sit out in the sun,
But now it just cannot be done.
The dangers there are all too true,
Now the harmful rays get through.
The polar cap is melting down,
And very soon whole towns will drown.
Acres of trees are wantonly felled,
The land turned into a barren hell.
The sea is fished too much it seems,
We are oblivious to nature's screams.
The soil is full of pesticides,
Where insects either die or hide.
And rivers where we swam and played,
Are poisoned now so stay away.
Why can't we stop and look and listen,
Before our world turns into a prison.
With barren land and empty skies,
Where nothing lives just rots and dies.
Please hope we close this destructive gate,
And put things right before it's too late.
Patricia Barber

Echoes of Yesterday
Gas lamps shine on cobbled streets here,
Where life was simple and sometimes austere.
In back to back houses with outside loo,
Black leaded grates and coal fires too.

We got on with our lives without much cause,
And were fed, clothed, and learned the three Rs.
The things we did when I was a boy,
With my best friend, who was called Roy.

No school after Friday, what a treat,
We could play all day in the street.
Those games we played, so long ago,
Marbles, whip and top and rallyvo.

There were times I would go with my pal,
For a walk alongside of the old canal.
And if you had sixpence you could get,
A bamboo cane, and on the end of a net.

With a warning from *Mum*, not to go far,
We would take a tin, or a large jam jar.
But to catch a glimpse of the dark scale carp,
Your eyes had to be so very sharp.

There was the Saturday matinee what a rush,
It's no wonder they called it the penny crush.
To see *Flash Gordon,* and the evil *Ming,*
In those days the cinema was King.

Friendships were forged throughout those years,
With fun and laughter and not many tears.
Then losing contact, going separate ways,
Oh! those wonderful old salad days.
Albert Stuttard

May Day Horses
Do you remember the May Day Horses,
with brasses shining, and ribbons bright,
through manes and tails plaited,
coats brushed and gleaming,
black hooves, feathered fetlocks a brilliant white.

24

Every day horses, pulling coal carts or beer drays,
we seldom took notice, we saw them each day.
Now we line the pavements as they pass, so proudly,
heads nodding, plumes waving, a royal display.

Here comes our Coalman, his cart be-ribboned,
Soldier his horse stepping lively and proud.
Seeming to know that today he is special,
on May Day he's King, his subjects, the crowd.

We waved our streamers and shouted, 'There's Rosie,'
she belongs to the milkman, a plump chestnut brown.
Bells on her collar, she trots on the cobbles,
red, white and blue, are the plumes in her crown.

May Day was special, we danced round the maypole,
sang songs to the lass who was Queen of the May.
But May Day to me meant the horses parading,
with brasses agleam, knowing it was their day!
Gladys Ross

The Ballad of a Bloxwich Pub
A simple little corner, aer pub the bell.
If yo live round blogsidge, then yo must know it well.
There's Bill the gaffer, Tum, Dick and Arry too,
B'rooh warra gaerm We 'av, when gooin to the loo.
We snake round the corner, in the rern an the snow.
An when we drop aer t rousers, the wind it doh arf blow.
Mah missus copped me one night, ooh warra fuss.
I'm angin arry aaht, she's sittin on the bus.
I mean, er day know it were me, er couldn't see me faerce,
But when I gor hum that night, er day arf cre'aert.
'Yo've bin up the Bell,' Er said. 'I aye I've bint the Prince.'
'Yo was angin in the lavvy, me faerce it day arf wince.'
Well er told er maerts abaht me, we ad quite afuss,
But guarantee on Friday night, tham sittin on the bus.

25

Nah think about it banks', Warrif the Queen should come,
An say er's tourin Blogsidge, I think we'd all goo hum.
There's Philip there, took quite short an pops in for a wee,
He's sittin nicely on the throne, for everyone to see.
We aye all posh round Blogsidge, but we luv that little bell,
Give us some nice loos Banks', Cus ow'er wives just give us ell.
Kate Gould

My Walking Stick

The path is slippery today,
The snow lies deep and thick;
How glad I am to lean upon
My sturdy walking stick.

It gives me confidence to take
The daily path I step on;
And in attack it yet could prove
A very handy weapon.

Its handle has an eagle head
Of finely moulded brass.
If dogs look menacing I raise
It slightly as they pass.

And here come schoolboys all armed with
Snowballs at the ready,
And dodging them, without my stick,
Would make me quite unsteady.

I use it to salute my pals
When I am walking out.
Ah yes, my stick is now a friend
I could not be without.
Iris Poole

Remember
This life we live is uncertain,
Tomorrow may never be here,
So try to spread some happiness,
At the start of another New Year,
Making someone smile and say 'Hello.'
Will give yourself that little glow.
Being there when someone needs you,
To tell their troubles to.
Will make your living so worthwhile,
Turning their grey skies to blue.
Don't say those things you might regret.
Then cannot make amends.
For who can tell when you may need,
That sincere, and loving friend.
So always count your blessings,
In everything you do,
For in giving, instead of taking,
Someone will always love you.
Jean Wicks

Our Land
Do you care about our countryside?
Do you care about our land?
Can you walk the hills in safety?
Is our world just as God planned?

There are folks who would destroy it,
There are those who just don't care
If the waters gets polluted
And have no time to stand and stare.

There are those who drop their litter
Causing danger where sheep graze,
There are folk, whose thoughtless actions
Can begin a fearful blaze.

27

Do you care about the countryside?
Do you care about this land?
Can you walk the moors in safety?
And enjoy the sea and sand?

Yes - we care about our countryside,
Yes - we care about our land.
And we'll walk the hills in safety
And enjoy all that God pianned.
Peggy Feltham

The Guilt is Equal

I swim in crimson waters
In fear of silver hooks,
I am the final whale
I survive in children's books.
I saw the scarlet coastline
Where the bleeding, dying lay,
I saw the foaming white tops
Where the youngest used to play.
I saw the bravest whaler
Hanging starboard over sea,
Gripping hold to harpoon gun
Its blooded sights on me.
I saw the sickening spittle
From his rasping yellow breath,
Screaming out instructions
To order out my death.
I know of man's opinions
And of his choice to fight
But who the hell is listening
When it comes to my life's rights?
I see no future hopefulness
Inside, I hold my fears,
From writer's pen to reader's eye
Their guilt alongside tears.

Vince Marsden

My Mom
My mom is very funny,
She often makes me laugh
When we go to the park
She gets on the swing and goes oh so high
Here I stand as I gasp and sigh.

She gets on the slide and goes whizzing down
The smile on her face
Reminds me of a clown.

We play hide and seek!
She'll hide behind the trees
And when I can't see her anywhere in sight
She'll jump out behind me and give a fright.

She gets on her knees and says she's looking for bees
People stop and stare to see why she
Has twigs in her hair.
But my mom just doesn't care.

She shouts, 'Let's run up the hill!'
And says, 'First one to the top is brill!'
We race along and I get there first.
She gasps and groans and says this is
No good for my old bones.

She sits down and laughs and says she had
a lot of fun.
And I think my mom is a great chum.
Yvonne McCracken

On Choosing the Family Pet
By brother, Joe, said, 'I know,
What about a rhino?'
Mum looked at him in the eye, 'No,
I'd fret for the kitchen lino.'

29

She's lucky - I *could* have picked a
Cuddly boa constrictor,
Probably called him Victor -
Victor the boa constrictor . . .

Mum callously refused me
Piranha fish in the jacuzzi.
Didn't think she was *that* choosy,
She picked Dad in an Excuse-Me!

Then Joe thought of a bison.
'Great, Joe,' I said. 'Nice one.'
Dad frowned, 'Wouldn't be wise, son.
Zap the lawn in a trice, son.'

I suggested a nice gorilla
Gran said the idea didn't thrill her.
Called to mind an old flame called Attila.
Big chap - supported the Villa.

The neighbours couldn't ignore us,
If we kept a brontosaurus,
Or a parrot called Delores,
Who could screech 'The Anvil Chorus'.

We rejected a chimp and a panda
(And a skunk to keep on the veranda)
Then, solution from Auntie Miranda -
A gerbil with delusions of grandeur!
Anita Hallett

The Retirement
Land of the rising sun
It rises in the east
Sets in the west
These are the days
That I love best.

30

Roses bloom, the gardens grow
Twelve noon on the old lilo
Warm hazy, lazy days
Hear how the music plays,
Lazy days doing your thing
Listening to the birdies' sing
Silver bird flying high
Flying high in the sky,
Apples green on the orchard bough
If only my friends could see me now.

I say that's awfully rude
Silly Billy it's only a boob
Me thinks I'll have a tipple
Put a little cream on that nipple
Roses Red got an aphid
Dearie me I've stripped Jack naked.
Hilda Bray

The End of the Road
What an unhealthy road we travel in 1993,
It has been clear for quite some time,
But not too plain to see.
We go along in cars and trucks
On every road in town,
And all the muck that we create
Could surely spare a frown.
For all the asthmatics that we know,
And they know they are many,
Their health is precious to us and them, and
Costs more than a pretty penny.
It's time for public transport again to be discussed.
Regular service, cheaper fares, healthier air,
Not to be rebuffed.

See for yourself if you will, travel along in that slow rush-hour,
We cannot keep putting traffic on roads,
That are beyond our power.
To build and mend as it's been done
For twenty years and more,
Eventually we will run out of motorway countryside for sure.
Ask the babes in ten more years
How many weak chests we've got,
We know it makes sense to say to traffic,
It's time to call a stop!
Sheila K Mulligan

The Right to Live
Long is the time since man's first birth
Then on he came to join with earth
To steep the earth with lust and greed
Thousands starve while others feed,
He fills our streams with toxic waste
And hopes it does not taste
He loads the earth with fumes and sprays
Well tested these, or so he says.
Who gives him right to maim, to kill?
When does he stop, when all is still?
He's here to take but not to give
And has he more right to live
Than Mother Nature's chosen few?
The right to live is theirs too
Would shooting still be such a fun
If mammal too could point a gun,
When in the end his doom begins
Will he answer to his sins
Or will he find he's just too late?
And find himself at hell's front gate
When he's destroyed all that's there
Then God will know he didn't care

32

When all's wiped out He'll start again
With animals instead of men,
Think as we head for Armageddon's end
Is man to earth a foe or friend?
Gordon Myers

Regrets

If I could but relive my life,
We hear people say;
I wouldn't make the same mistakes
That I made yesterday.

The money that I squandered.
The chances that I missed.
The wrong paths that I wandered.
The wrong lips that I kissed.

The harsh words swiftly spoken,
Which cost me a dear friend.
A heart so quickly broken,
And so very slow to mend.

The letters that I didn't write;
Which might have meant so much.
Too late, was I to see the light?
I wish I'd kept in touch.

All of these things I'd surely change,
We hear people say;
If only I'd known yesterday,
What I know today.

But human nature doesn't change,
The way that we are, we stay.
And the mistakes that we made yesterday,
We could make again, today.
Tom Taylor

Dear John

I'm sorry John this is the end
For you always look a mess,
I despise your greasy dandruff
And the grotty way you dress.
I loathe the blackheads and the spots
That surround your chin and nose,
Your breath is foul just like your feet
And your socks expose your toes!
You reek of sweat, your teeth are black
Your fingernails are so grimy,
You've got big ears and a double chin
And your kisses are all slimy.
It's no good, John, my mind's made up
I'd like to make the break,
What's that, John, you've won the pools
And you're sure there's no mistake?
Well really, John! You should have said,
Of course we'll name the day,
We'll rush right round to the Registrar
And get wed right away.
Just pay no heed to what I've said,
Of course I love you, Honey,
I only hope that folk won't think
That I'm marrying you for money!

Marlene Rowley

Desolation

Autumn now is here.
Leaves fall down
Swirling all around.
My heart is sore,
I cannot bear this sad pain.

34

Autumn now is here.
Rain falls down,
Tears are falling fast.
My heart will break,
I cannot bear this sad pain.

Where are you, my love?
Where are you?
I long to hold your hand,
I long to kiss your lips.

Happiness was ours,
Deep, strong love.
Happy summer days
When we first met,
Our love a taste of heaven's bliss.
Joy was in my heart,
Strong my love.
Was our love to last
Sweet summer love?
We thought we'd love forever,
Our youth untried as yet.
The world's a cruel place
And ecstasy's for heaven.

Winter now is here,
Snow falls down
Swirling all around.
My heart will break.
There's winter in my sad soul.
Heather Middleton

The Harvest
Plough till the land lies
in brown waves of loam
Plough on until you find
your own sweet home.

Plough even though you trip
over pebbles and bricks
Plough on regardless
of all life's tricks.

Plough to where your heart sings
vibrant and free
Plough till you find the place
where you dream to be.

Then sow all of your dreams
in the place where you rest
and make a reality
of things you love best.

Then reap in your harvest
that's flowered in your ground
and rejoice in that glittering prize
that your labour has found.

S Booth

Winter at School

Each of the seasons reveals its own beauty,
Bringing us joy at the endless display.
What will compare with the splendours of winter
Seen by us now in the course of each day?

Wonderful patterns of frost on the windows,
Brightness and cold, not a cloud in the sky.
Trees with bare branches and snow-covered hedges,
Shouts of delight as the children go by.

Dazzle of white from the snow on our playground,
Infinite heaven a delicate blue.
Tingle of winter in mind and in body,
Making us eager in all that we do.

Snow settled firmly at afternoon playtime,
Warmth of the sunshine, so shortly to yield.
Crunching of ice and whizzing of snowballs,
Gardens and poplars alongside the field.

Treetops ablaze as the sun sinks behind them,
Spires rising high in the vanishing light.
Welcoming glow of our homes and our firesides,
Glittering stars in the darkness of night.

Each of the seasons reveals its own beauty,
Bringing us joy at the endless display.
What will compare with the splendours of winter
Seen by us now in the course of each day?

This poem is published by courtesy of the Essex Education
Committee, in whose magazine *Essex Education* it originally
appeared.
David Hewitt

Lorna-Winter
Why reflect again?
Thoughts of her history
Are immobile to my eye.
Yet I lament for Lorna,
Her crown thin and poor, like hairs
On an old wart.
She bared her soul,
Even as deciduous branches bare themselves
under snow.
Through a cloudy maze of time,
She changes not her place,
Though eternity grows aimless.

Lorna, I trace your image
On a sea of thoughts.
Bereft of debris and doubts,
I caress your calm and
Easy sleep.
John Pearce

Waiting

Come into my dreams
And stay a little while
Do not fade away
Until I've seen your sunny smile.

For the day ahead
Will be bleak and bare
Knowing when I awake
You will not be there.

I long to hold
And to touch
Is it asking too much
For I miss you, and love you I do.

I cling to my pillow
And wish it were you
I remember your eyes
So vividly blue.
My own fill with tears
Looking back through the years
When war took you
And left me with fears.

Longing and waiting for your return
When again we'll wander through the fern
Two happy people
With memories galore
Never to wander from England's shore.
Olga Male

Lonely Rain

We love to sit in the sun and feel its warming rays,
To dream that there's begun a wealth of summer days,
When long will be the hours of day and short the night,
Gloom can be forgotten and everything looks bright.

But do we care to walk in the rain along a shining street,
And down a muddy lane, or listen to the beat
Of raindrops on the roof insisting constantly,
Put on your waterproof, come out and walk with me.

The sun has many friends but lonely is the rain,
As we are drawn to joy and shy away from pain.
Thus life itself's a mixture of happenings good and bad,
The sunshine and the showers, the happy and the sad.

So, in joy, are we not prone to leave the sad to walk alone?
Phyllis Holden

Our Charlotte

Me grandchild's bawling, she's not got her dolly,
We're popping into Sainsburys, must grab a trolley.
The reason I've got her, her mum needs a rest,
God, this child's putting my nerves to the test.
One tin of beans Charlotte not flipping four,
I'll be glad when we're finished and get out the door.
Down the next aisle, we look for the jam,
Charlotte by now is eating some spam.
I rescue the packet and explain I'll pay later,
I bump into a trolley and there's an almighty clatter.
That's it, that's enough, as I clean up the mess,
Your granny's getting old and you couldn't care less.
I get her home and give her her tea,
There's a special bond between her and me.
I put her to bed and kiss her goodnight,
I thank God we've got her and put out the light.
Mary Wilkinson

Troubles

We only have one life to live
To make the best of things
None of us are angels
And none of us have wings.

So why must we both try to be
Something we are not
Why can't we get on with life
And be happy with our lot.

We always seem to quarrel
And always seem to fight
No matter what I try to do
It never turns out right.

If I could have just one wish
I'd turn my life around
I'd try to be a different soul
With both feet on the ground.

There are times when things are peaceful
And everything's just right
Then all at once the balloon goes up
And we're back into a fight.

Things should be better, you must agree
At our time in life
I suppose our troubles are meant to be
After all, we're man and wife.
A Baxter

Ode to Matthew James

Flesh of my flesh,
Great joy to me in all the earth.
Babe of my child,
To whom those years ago I did give birth.

With downy head,
Sweet shell-like ears and tiny feet
and pearly nails,
A perfect miniature complete.
So through the years,
When all is said and done,
I'll always hold you dear to me,
Son of my son.
Edna Robinson

Untitled

Will you walk with me once again
Down country road and winding lane?
Listen to the birds refrain
Enjoy the breath of spring.

We will stroll through meadows and
See the things that nature planned
The sun is shining, it's so grand
To see toadstools in fairy rings.

As summer sun sits on high
We could walk you and I
Happy as the days go by
Watching birds upon the wing.

In autumn we will walk again
Down that shady, leafy lane
The leaves now brown but don't complain
That is the established thing.

Though alone I walk these days
The beauty of life I always praise
For nature in so many ways
Makes my heart sing.
Richard J Illingworth

Night Wind

Why! I can smell the hay quite clear
In this dark garden hour!
And thoughts of sun and hay so near
Dispel all other moments drear
That make this life so sour.

I hear the rustle in the trees,
Stare at the clear-blown sky.
I never thought till I heard these
Of all the magic in the leaves
And in the night wind's cry.

The full moon hangs there bright and still
An oasis of light
To dark, benighted traveller still
Enchanting with its radiance till
I wonder at the night.

The black, stark shadows moonlight weaves
So unfamiliarly!
And free and cool from all the seas
The chill fresh bluster of the breeze -
Ah loves! You call to me!
Don Panting

Town

The shopping centre is a busy place
People running to and fro
Trying to find a familiar face
I've been here for an hour or so.

There's women pushing chairs
With little babies in
I have to use the moving stairs
To avoid the awful din.

42

In and out of shops all day
Trying to find what I need
Such a queue when it comes to pay
So I go somewhere else for speed.

People running, rushing around
The choirs doing a display
They make a very lovely sound
As they sing away.

Congestion and pollution out on the streets
As the cars fill up the road
The market man selling meats
Shouting out to sell his load.

Now it's time to get away
I have bought my new black comb
I will come back another day
But now I'm going *home!*
Linda Ram (13)

Love

Love is a dew on a bloom
Love is a breeze in summer
Love is a ripple of water
Love is two in one!

Love commences at birth
Love is with us forever
Love doesn't end with death
Love lives on!
L I Weren

The Metaphorical Burglar

Dog tired, the cat burglar, arrived back at his house
He crept through to the kitchen, as quiet as a mouse.
As hungry as a horse and as greedy as a hog
He ate like a pig, then he slept like a log

Though cunning as a fox and as strong as an ox
He was as mild as a lamb to his wife and their tots
He was proud as a peacock of his wife and the children
And would fight like a tiger, if anyone illed them

He began his career to support his first daughter
And he took to like a duck takes to water
His wife turned a blind eye to his illegal pickings
And she treated the children like a hen with her chickens

He was lively as a cricket while the children were little
And he genuinely felt he was as fit as a fiddle
Though stubborn as a mule to any thoughts of a change
He was wise as an owl, although this may sound strange

He was blind as a bat to his uncertain future
And at the time never considered agriculture
But as he grew older, the thought was alarming
So he decided to settle for animals and farming.
Morton Rock

Loneliness

I sit alone, the hours go by,
Must I sit here until I die?
No-one to hear, no-one to speak,
The future is now looking bleak,
I think again about my past,
A smile comes on my face at last,
I think of all the fun I've had,
Fun that was good, none of it bad.

Good friends I had, though some are dead,
Remembering names when I'm in bed
Of girls at school and often smile
About corridors we walked in single file,
Of boys who made a noise upstairs,
Going to the hall to join in prayers.
The teachers too were awfully kind,
A better crowd would be hard to find.
We all left school with, 'I'll be in touch,'
The weeks went by, we didn't write much.
Some found jobs in far off places,
I forget their names but remember faces.
Sometimes a photo will appear
In local papers over the year.
And then I'll think, I knew him well,
He used to toll the old school bell.
Where are these friends who used to be,
Are they as lonely, just like me?
Anne Schmidt

Miss you
The birds sit on the windowsill
Waiting to be fed
We're all behind this morning
Stayed too long in bed.

The house has lost its smile today
The clouds have drowned the sun
Time is standing still
Now we're without our Mum.

The flowers in the garden
Turn their faces to the ground
The blackbird's stopped his singing
Now Mother's not around.

When you went away
You said, 'I won't be long!'
But you've been gone for years and years
And years are far too long.

Now looking from our window
What is this I see?
Could it be our Mum
Returning home to me?

It's great to have you back Mum
You've been missed in many ways
We've had a job to manage
You've been gone, two, whole, days.
Brian Partner

Thoughts of You

As I sit in my four walled room
Without you my life is full of gloom
As I think of you, I feel I'm falling apart
I think once more, and you lift up my heart.
You are the one that I love
You mean more to me than the sky above
And so my darling don't you see
There'll never ever be anyone else for me.
Elizabeth Jane Rice

Depression

You feel lonely and need company
And yet you want to be alone
Everything seems too much trouble
Life seems to have no reason
You plod on day after day
Wondering who cares - if anyone does

46

You want to feel joy, but all there is, is sorrow
You hope maybe things will change tomorrow.
There seems to be something, someone missing
You wonder what it is?
Then you realise, maybe it's love and companionship.
Sharon Poppe

Emma

My mind is blank
We knew each other so well
I knew your thoughts
You broke my heart,
I cried for days
I still cry for you
We all cry for you
You were loved
You still are
You're in my heart.
We'll never part
You were so kind
Your eyes are on my mind,
You were so perfect
Flawless in every way
When God made you
No-one stood in His way.
You'll never be replaced
No-one can ever take your place
I'll see you again one day.
Christine Baran

A Childhood Memory

'Twas in the springtime long ago
When I was just a child
At lunchtime I came out of school
The weather it was mild,

47

I hurried off down by the farm
To see if celandines were out
They were, oh what joy they brought
It made me laugh and shout.
To other children passing by
They were as pleased as me
We all loved the springtime
With so much new to see,
In those days of wartime
When things were in short measure
We made the most of God's great gifts
To give us daily pleasure.
Joyce E Strong

Childhood Memories

I think of childhood, and a magic stirs within me,
On memory's back I ride to times most dear,
      Nostalgia calls to mind,
      Halcyon days left far behind,
And a longing for those days of yesteryear.

The joy of paddling where the stream was shallow,
The gentle lap of water round my feet,
      Playing in the hay,
      And at the close of day
To ride home on the haycart was a treat.

Skipping through the fallen leaves in autumn,
Reading in the lamplights' gentle glow,
      Hot cocoa, dripping toast,
      were the things I liked the most,
After walking home from school midst falling snow.

A visit to the village shop seemed oh so special
A ha'penny was all I'd have to spend
  The choice of sweets was many
  Four ounces for a penny
And I'd search the row of jars from end to end.

Golden days of childhood, how I loved them
May the solace that they bring me long remain
  My twilight reverie
  Brings back such memories to me
And in my heart I am a child again.
Joan Thomson

The Memory Tree

When at first I saw the tree
the leaves were dark and red,
reminding me of two world wars
and blood that had been shed.

The cold winds blew the leaves away
making the branches twist and sway,
like soldiers standing firm their ground
with a battle raging all around.

Spring had come when I looked again
I saw new buds swell in the rain,
life had sprung fresh from the tree
like new recruits in the infantry.

All the buds were true to form
matching colours in uniform,
the buds grew strong and turned to leaves
shining like medals one had achieved.

It's summer now and peace not war
the leaves and branches sway no more,
the soldiers all have fought their best
the battle done now they will rest.

How wonderful to see a tree
and recall to mind the memory
of brave men who gave up their lives
so as their country should survive.
Valerie Evans

The Course of True Love
The course of true love
Never runs smooth
With good comes bad
With happiness comes blues.
When you're alone
Lying in your bed
A mass of thoughts
Flying through your head,
The one thought that stands
Clear and true is
The course of true love
Never runs smooth.
Alan R Woodrow

Far Away
For all the people up above, here's
A few words to the ones we love
Far away, so far away we will all
be with you one day, you know we
think of you every day in our
dreams and in our own way, so
to all our loved ones up above,
we shall not worry because we know
you have God's love.
H J Thwaites

The Voyage of Souls

There is a great sea before us
It's name, Disillusioned Bay,
Where the souls of the unhappy
Choose to spend their final day.

All know how to reach there
But none do yet return
Only the memories of the departed
Remain for us to yearn.

Now as I sail towards there,
The flame of life doused within
The day of judgement dawns upon me
Do I sink, or shall I swim?

The salty taste of my tears
Stain my face as they flow
As I sink toward oblivion
In the dark waters below.

So do not grieve for me my friends
And do not mourn me on this day
Should you reach the port of the disillusioned
Hoist anchor and calmly sail away.
A C Jones

The Apple Tree

I am an apple tree living in earth,
Standing so tall from that pip at my birth.
Roots spreading below and boughs reaching out
From this spot where I stand with grass all about.
What I need for my life and to help me to grow
Comes through my roots from far down below.
Sunrays pour down to warm me all through,
Dust washed from my leaves by the rain and the dew.

Birds give me their music and men give me praise,
Nights sheds her coolness after hot summer days.
The wind undresses me and away my leaves blow,
Winter gives me her sleep under a blanket of snow.
I need take no thought or ask for a thing,
For all is done for me from something within.

All these good things toward me are driven,
Now hear the good things that from me are given.

My roots hold the granules of soil all together,
And I shelter the small life in all sorts of weather.
All kinds of people receive joy from my form,
For artists, pink blossom the blue sky adorn
And bees receive nectar to put in their hive
That man may have honey and the swarm stay alive.
I give health to all through my apples to eat
When they are ripened and rosy and juicy and sweet.
Birds rest on my twigs on a passage of flight,
And small boys climb up me and laugh with delight.
My foliage gives shade to those feeling hot,
And I announce all the seasons and forget them not.
I am called apple tree and you are called man,
But both of us live in the *I* that I am.
Veronica Rowlands

My Holiday 1961
Gorleston early in the morning,
Brushing teeth, it won't take long,
Wake up sister, you'll miss breakfast,
Hurry up, there goes the gong.

At the table eating crisp's,
Spilling sugar on the floor,
Here comes Charles in with the bacon,
Daddy, I can eat no more.

Off to wooden hut on sea front,
Riding ponies on the sands,
Candy floss and salted peanuts,
Ice cream cones and sticky hands.

Dip my tootsies in the water,
After walking on those stones,
More ice cream and toffee apples,
Should put flesh upon my bones.

Off to dinner at the Cranbrook,
Soup and fish and crepe suzette,
Spilling coffee on my sun suit,
Should have used my serviette.

Mummy may I leave the table,
I do not like this fruit and cream,
May we stay up late this evening,
There's a show we haven't seen.

After dinner and the toilet,
All along the front we strut,
Mum and I we walk on slowly,
Josephine and Daddy putt.

In my lower bunk at night-time,
Sister bouncing overhead,
Yet another day tomorrow,
I feel so tired I could be dead.
Reginald Biggs

Inside Out
On the outside
Man of the world
Inside
A child,
In fear of commitment
Love
Life.

On the outside
Laughing at adversity
Inside
Scared to death,
That one day he'll be
Found
Out.

On the outside
Happy to be alive
Inside
Welcoming any excuse,
To hide away until it's
All
Over.

On the outside
Wearing well
Inside
Wearing out.
Fred Wright

A Friend
'Give me a shoulder to cry on, when a crisis looms into view,
Tell me, that on the horizon, the sun will come shining through.

Join me, in tears of laughter, share with me, my happiness,
Tell me, I'm looking attractive, when my hair is a terrible mess.

Insist that my diet is working, although you can see it is not!
Encourage me, when I am shirking, not caring what shape I
have got.

Send me a card on my birthday, but don't you dare mention my age!
Loan me the book you are reading, before you reach the last page.

Gossip about me to others, but be sure what you say is true,
Give me advice on my problems, but *don't* tell me what to do!

Give me a lift when it's raining, or lend me a mac, when I'm soaked.
Listen, when I keep complaining, and lend me a pound when
I'm broke.

Come visit me, seldom or often, but be sure not to make any fuss,
When removing the toys, from the cushion and please turn a
blind eye to the dust!

When I boast of my children, please listen, and praise all the
gifts they possess,
Congratulate me, on their achievements and agree they are
brought up the best!

Care, when I'm world worn and weary and my back is
beginning to break.
Sympathise, with the rest of my ailments and listen to all of
my aches.

A friend, you can ask any favours, is a friend that is faithful and true,
To put up with all faults and all failures, may I be, such a friend to
you.'

Sheila Mary Smith

I Love My Mum

I love my mum, the little child said,
I loved my nan: now she is dead.
I love my teddy who's lost an eye,
Though he's old and tatty, he will never
            go away or die.

I love my friend who plays with me
He's the bestest friend a friend could ever be.
His father's black, his mother's white,
But he's taught him how to fly his kite.

But I do love my mum - she is alright,
And when she cries I hug her tight.
For I know that makes her sad, you see,
It's because she cannot find a proper
            Dad for me.

I told my mum 'it ain't that bad,
Why should you upset yourself and be sad,
When there are children without mother, father
            friend or toy,
All in all, I'm a very lucky boy'.
Robert McKenzie

To My Widow

After sitting alone at the close of day
your ageing body weary, hair now all grey,
Across the fields you hear a curlew cry
as you climb the stairs with a weary sigh.

When you lie in your bed cold and alone
with no one left to share hearth and home,
Think of your husband who loved you so dear
and feel warm as you draw your memories near.

Remember your man who so happy you made
and let your pains and cares slowly fade,
Remember our love as we hugged every night
and smiled at each other in morning light.

As a moonbeam shines across your lonely bed
remember the words of love your man said,
Then go to sleep with a contented smile
knowing he watches over you all the while.

You know one night whilst peacefully asleep
the moonbeam a predestined date will keep,
One night it will let your spirit run free
and gently carry you from your bed to me.
Malcolm Craig

Time Off

Amid the hustle and bustle,
of the human race,
do you ever stop and look?
and slow down on the pace.

Just try it now and then,
and find the beauty all around,
It's surprising, what you can find,
take the time off, look around.

There are other things in life
apart from work and making money,
The beauty of the flowers and trees
the bee's so busy making honey.

So, take time off, enjoy it,
there's so much you can gain,
for the hustle and the bustle
will only bring you pain.

The beauty is there all around,
it's there for you and me,
Enough of it for everyone,
and it's absolutely free.
E C Dye

My Brother

My brother is a pain,
he splashes in the rain,
he gets me wet and then
he says he wants a pet,
he makes a noise
when I am trying to think,
and then he says he wants a drink,
as you can see my brother
is a pain for me
and my mum
that one.
Aimi Mulligan (7)

Life's Treasure

I had seventy years to spend, golden guineas every one
Plus a little dividend for when my life was nearly done.

Having such a splendour store is an honour worth its price?
Would a fortune please me more? Would just happiness suffice.

Let the purchaser beware lest he waste his golden pence
On nothing else than empty air, flavoured with experience.

Here a guinea spent with care after long and careful thought
Left me stunned and in despair, far from pleased with what it
                                        brought.

There a guinea spent in haste when I found the subject boring
Left my enemies disgraced, and my reputation soaring.

Here a guinea gained a friend, there a guinea lost the lot.
Now I've nearly reached the end. Whether wisely spent or not
What I've done I can't amend. I must live with what I've got.
Ralph Clarke

Our World

As we look on to the future,
We worry what it will be,
Or even if we shall still be around,
Because of what we are doing,
To our precious and unique world,
With all the problems,
The wars and the fights,
The ozone layer,
The pollution of rivers and roads,
Soon we shall all be looking like zombies,
Our animals are dying,
So to is the earth,
Which God has made,
If he could see us, what would he think
Of his beautiful world?
Being turned into a rubbish dump,
This must stop as,
We will have no world to live in,
Our grandchildren,
What hope do they have?
When the price of everything.
Is too high to pay,
And there are no jobs around,
In years to come,
I wonder what will,
Happen to this world at the end,
When us humans have,
Destroyed it all.
Claire L Philpott

Poetry Now
Freedom of thought, contained within.
Never disclosed to man or kin,
Flights of fancy to reach the heights,
Thoughts of despair, in shaken dislike.

Freedom of thoughts in speech and in action,
In sport and at work, to see the reaction.
Freedom of thoughts, a dangerous subject,
For it confronts the adverse public.

Guard your mind and guard your tongue,
Guard your day, before it's begun,
Never speak your mind to anyone you meet,
Just mention the weather, oh, what a relief.

Freedom of thought is a delicate subject,
It leads you among people with different objectives
If you want to feel safe, be diplomatic,
'Good morning, fine day' it's automatic.

The real you no one ever knows,
It's locked inside you and never comes out
It's hidden well, contained within,
It's not even shared among your kin.

The real you is private and precious to you,
The real you is something you only knew,
Locked up inside you, hidden well,
It's taken with you on your final farewell.
Elizabeth Anna Powley

Me
Life's a bitch and then you die
or so they say
events are made to happen
experience is something to be learned.

60

Life is for the living
and I intend to do just that
with all I know
with all I have
each day's a new beginning
each nights a restful place
birth, death, an everyday thing
work is stressful.
Motherhood's a headache
unemployment's a dark and lonely place
laughter's a tonic.
Love's a nice place to be,
Talking's a skill,
Life's full of knowledge,
This is the place for me
My life's great
I'm glad,
I'm me.

Julie Leathers

The Lonely Listener

I hear a tiny dripping noise! It's my kitchen tap
and my neighbours cat purring, sitting on my lap
the kitchen clock ticking, the fridge gently humming
thought I heard footsteps, but found no one was coming.
I hear some tiny snowflakes tapping my window pane
and listen for those footsteps, once again in vain
I listen for the postman, putting letters through the box
But a double glazing salesman is the only one who knocks
Purring, dripping, ticking and humming!
Elusive footsteps, but no one coming
It could be worse, I could be deaf, hear no sound at all
And miss those taps on my window pane, as the snowflakes
                                                    gently fall.

Norman Neild

Friend

You knew my thoughts without a word
I didn't speak . . . and yet you heard
You saw the pain within my mind . . .
That others always fail to find.

You saw because you'd been there too . . .
And did what no one else could do . . .
You gave me comfort in despair
Knowing, friend, that you'd been there.

I saw reflections in your eyes
Of myself, my thoughts, that old disguise,
A mirrored image of that me
That only one the same could see.

And friend in this cruel world of sorrow,
I will be there, today, tomorrow
To comfort . . . help you bear the load
Lean on me friend, on life's long road.
And I will bear the weight, the strain
That you may carry me again.
Jean Farrow

My Old Dad

My old dad is a pigeon man
He only keeps a few.
Maybe about a dozen hens
And a cock bird to keep them true.

At one time he had a very big team
But he found it didn't pay
Because the work involved, was far too great
So he had fo find an easier way.

62

At first he got rid of the old birds
Then the second day ones as well
All the pretty ones, got a good going over
And the difference at a glance you could tell.

I was the one who mucked them out
About two hours every day
But now it takes only half an hour
And I'm hoping it keeps that way.

The lady birds are paired together
They each have a box called home.
And when the time is ready,
The big cock, is allowed to roam.

Now the birds are very successful
Since my dad started to race this way
Only six birds are sent to each race
Because jealously seems to help you could say.

At weekends, when the birds are racing
I help to scan the sky.
Hoping my dad gets a good one,
As you can spot them, as they come by.

Then it's all a matter of trapping
But my dad had thought that out
He had trained his birds, to fly to his hand,
So anytime he could lose was nought.

The most my dad clocked, was two birds
He said it was unfair to clock more
After all it was a sport for all to enjoy
For to clock others, would become a bore.

Now if you be a pigeon fancier
And your racing is getting you down
Do like my old dad did
Then one day, you could wear a crown.
Raymond Gallagher

Why?

Why is the world so violent?
When so much beauty abounds.
Why can't men live in peace?
And enjoy what they see all around,
Why can't all creeds live in harmony?
Why do some need to plant bombs
What pleasure is there knowing someone is dead?
Why oh why are these people so cruel?
Why are such deeds disguised as religion?
This cannot be what it's about.
God meant us to love one another
Not maim and mutilate.
O E Barber

The Gift of Life

The gift of life is special,
So you two must be special too,
To be given this son to cherish,
From all the trouble he'll put you through.

Having this baby meant the world to you,
To complete your happiness,
I hope he brings you joy and laughter,
And in his nappies loads of mess.

I see him at only an hour old,
A tiny bundle of joy,
And I see in your eyes the love you'd give,
To this beautiful baby boy.

His features are immaculate,
Having Mark's nose is not a sin,
But the most exquisite feature of all,
Is the dimple in his chin.

This baby will be loved by you,
And treasured with all your might,
Mark and Pearl you are now the proud parents of,
Taylor, Mark Lee Wright.
Kerry Pentecost

If Life
If life don't seem to go right
We should
Not get down but stand up and fight.

If life never seems calm
We should
Not worry and cause more alarm.

If life doesn't appear good
We should
Ask ourselves is my path understood.

If life don't give us what we need
We should
Think back to our planted seed.

If life always looks bad
We should
Be curious was it ours what we had.

If life isn't much fun
We should
Maybe walk instead of run.

If life is just one big struggle
We should
See what areas we can juggle.

If life's dreams never seem met
We should
Realise what we put in is what we get.

If life don't seem to change
We should
Plan the parts of ourselves we can rearrange.

If life seems like a wheel
We should
Ask is it because the way we feel.
Karen Holman

I Remember Parliament Street (1959)

We used to live in a back to back house
Just me ma and me,
Wi' one room up and one room darn'
And an outside lavatory.
Newspaper squares tied one with string
With a long drop toilet, I hated that thing
Splinters in your backside
And scared of falling down,
No proper lock on the door
And nosy parkers hanging round.

We had an attic too wi' an 'ole it roof,
At night we'd watch the stars,
An old tin bath to catch the rain,
It used to be me ma's,
We had no wireless or telly
To help the evenings along,

We had an old piano,
At night we had a sing-song,
Gas mantles were our only light,
Plus an odd candle or so,
The mantles cost a bob apiece
I broke 'em so I ought to know.

In'sa they pulled 'em darn'
We got a council house in't tarn,
Oh it felt fairly posh wi' a bedroom to misel
But I'll never forget that back to back house,
As my memories will tell,
Where the old street stood now stands the police station
All grand and modern and new
So if you lived on Parliament Street
Then you should remember it too!
Susan Brierley

Childhood

There's a puddle down our street
On top floats a rainbow of oil
And bobbing gently up and down
There's a piece of silver foil.

He sits with his feet in the gutter
And wipes his nose on his sleeve
He looks at the pool and is lost
In a world of make believe.

Down a back entry a voice calls
Urging him home for tea
But he's sailed on a silver galleon
Across a jewelled sea.
Joyce Ball

Pictures From the Past

Hark I hear the elders singing
Reminiscent of the past
Good old days, the bells are ringing
      How long will nostalgia last?

Stiff collared gents stand oh, so haughty
Pictures of Victorian belles
The cancan they did was so naughty
      The debtors in their prison cells.

Well clad ladies in long dresses
Walk their children in the street
Buttoned boots and flowing tresses
      Begging urchins in bare feet.

Hail the Yule tide logs a-burning
In the old ancestial home
Sucking pigs on spits are turning
      Poached rabbit game enough for some.

Salute the brave wives and the mothers
Wave their men off to the war
Fighting side by side with brothers
      Poppies bloom forever more.

Ah - the pretty country cottage
Pictured on a sunny day
White haired couple in their dotage
      The workhouse is not far away.

A D James

Look Into My Eyes

Look into my eyes,
See what is inside, past my skin,
What is beyond my face,
The way I talk, walk or dress.

68

Look into my eyes,
See the harshness and cold,
Imperfections or perfectness of the shell,
Peel back the layers of my life.

Look into my eyes,
See the heartbreak, see the truth,
They will not tell you a lie,
For they are my true self, the way I feel.

Look into my eyes,
See the depth within my soul, tenderness of my heart,
Gaze at the joy, hate, love or greed,
All my thoughts I will impart.

Look into my eyes,
See what lies beneath the surface,
Kindness and consideration are not carried without,
But, look deep and you will understand.
V Chapman

Thoughtless Humans

As you enter and go into the lovely wood
Give a care for nature which little understood
When walking you are talking not caring to tread
Damaging insect life of which some will be dead.

When the sunshine rays pierce into the glade
You expect grass but you'll never see a blade
Those rotten boughs which are on the floor
Hold different kinds of life by the score.

No care is given for what lives there
Whatever noise you make is cause to scare
The birds which are many, some on nest
Trying to bring up their young like the rest.

So please let us try and be fair
To the trees and things that are there
They can't speak to say 'Leave us be'
Some humans do not care you see.
Renit

Reflections
Wouldn't it be good if you could turn back the past,
And undo all the bad things that happened so fast.
You wouldn't have done half the things that you did,
You wouldn't have hidden the things that you hid.
You wouldn't have hurt the people that care,
You wouldn't have hit out as though they weren't there.
The people you love wouldn't have suffered the pain,
The pain you've delivered again and again.
There wouldn't be sadness, tears and regrets
There wouldn't be moments loved ones try to forget.
Yet those bad things did happen, they happened so fast,
Those bad things that happened back there in the past.
Toni Wright

Cold and Lonely
Cold and lonely,
The heat drifting away,
To reveal the young boy,
In the dark and damp,
Holding the small, motionless
child in his arms,
Lifeless, no more cries,
Still,
A shiver,
Quiet,
Deathly and bitter
Waiting patiently,
for a rescuer.
Carrie Bloomfield (13)

Ode to Charlie (Grandad)

Your grandad died today
You know you should be sad,
I tried to cry but I could not
In fact it made me mad.

For in reflection of his life
A good one at the start,
It seems a shame, the living game
Is tearing them apart.

For what respect our old people
Where is their claim, to fame?
When the twilight years are here
In their homes they remain.

But what can they do
It's not safe for them no more,
Life is like a captive in a cage
Lock the window, bolt the door.

Your grandad died today
The tears should stain my face,
But somehow I wonder deep inside
That he's in a better place.
Lisa McMurtry

History

History's a mystery
Some things are still unknown
But as we pass each century
We find new history zones,
Some people find it boring
Others think it's great
The rest just take no bother
They just sit and hesitate.

It's happening while you read this
It's all around the globe
It stretches back a long, long time
To when people wore no clothes,
Everybody's in it
Nobody's left out
People read about it
And others shout it out.
Monarchs were all in it
Jesus Christ was too
So was Florence Nightingale
Who used to cure the flu,
Dick Turpin wasn't missed out
Neither was Robin Hood
They nicked things from the bad
And gave them to the good.
And now we are approaching
The climax of our song
I really am so sorry
That it wasn't very long
Becky Lord (13)

Storm of the Mind
A mighty storm approaches
Darkness descending to blot out light
O' foolish self to think it was past
That I could stand and fight
My soul cries out in despair
And hope withers away.

The siege of mind has began
Myself to find and victory to be won
Recapture me and triumph yet
But confused, bewildered, terror reigns
And still to conquer the prison of my shame.

Anger, rage, hate, inward turning
Answers clear and fearfully minded
Destruction, death, all consuming
When will I learn, me I must love.

Tearing, ripping, surely it's clear
Silent words that must be heard
My heart and mind are separated
Two answers always when one is needed.

And now the valley of decision
Which way am I to turn
For one is of life and one of death
But seeped out of me is my answer
Sucked dry and tired are my bones

What then of loved one stood before me
You suffer silently, through your eyes it gleams
I don't know what you see in me
How is it possible, a fool maybe?
But a tender understanding smile upon your face.

So can I now perceive with inner damaged eyes?
The answer that is in front of me
That love conquers all
And included is me.
Cathy Parkin

The Emperor's New Clothes
We paid our money gladly to admire
the graceful quivering, the shimmering
livery of the foreign butterflies,
dazzling as any courtier at Versailles
in finery of velvets, silks and golds.

Only a child observed the peasantry
outside, a mob of common ladybirds
who foraged, picking clean a bush and then
unfurled their folded wings of black and red
and flaunted flags of freedom to the world.
Pauline Simpson

For My Children (Ryan, Amy and Joseph)
Catch my daytime hand,
Step into tomorrow.
A touch of colour on your cheeks
Nestles in my soul.
Don't walk on the far side
Imagine, and try to understand
I am committed to your souls.
Everything I want to say
Will never be born or read
On paper;
The words melting in my mind
Long before they can be told.
Cling to what you see
Before you walk away.
As you will forever repeat
On stony grounds
Storms roll through me,
As I kneel beside you.
The tears I shed for you
Pass un-noticed.
Wherever you go in life
I will be thinking of you,
Hoping I can always guide you
To the right path back home.
Annie Lofkin

Gone to Seed

I had laid my table
My mother was coming to tea
But there was something missing -
Of course! No flowers to be seen
So I went into the garden
Hoping to find a few stray blooms
The storm had left behind
But sadly none had survived
So reluctantly and empty handed
I was going inside
When I saw on my vegetable patch
A splash of pink!
And there were my lovely flowers
Just waiting to be picked
I put them in a vase
And my table they enhanced!
My mother said, 'Such pretty flowers
What are they called?'
And with a smile I said
'Pretty flowers they are indeed
But they are only radishes
Gone to seed'

Edna Whittaker

Compassion

To think of other people can really be such fun
Better than all the time thinking of number one.
To do a friend a favour, to give someone a smile
The joy of their receiving can make it so worthwhile,
If you cannot do a good deed, never do a bad
There are enough things in the world to make one really sad.
So try with cheerful countenance to brighten up each day
And give help where it's needed as you go along the way
It really is the best thing that we can ever give
To give of ourselves to others for just as long as we live.
Evelyn Arnold

I am, am I?

I am a neo-nazi, a facist too,
or am I a black lesbian or a wealthy Jew
or am I a pregnant mother or a closet gay,
or am I just a victim, just another of your prey?

I am a Left Wing socialist, a hero of any cause,
or am I blind from birth or paralysed in the war
or am I a lonely granny or a small child at play
or am I just a victim, just another of your prey?

I am a teacher, a doctor, a nun,
or am I a child, a man, a wife on the run,
or am I homeless, a drunk or a stray
or am I just a victim, just another of your prey?

You may never know the answer,
I never had a chance to say,
As I fell like your victim,
just another of your prey?
Nicola Plumb

Sad World

The world outside
My window,
Feels very dark,
And bleak.
The secrets stored,
Inside my head,
No long I can keep.

I want to stop crying,
I want to be liked,
I want to be remembered,
For knowing wrong
From right.

I need someone to
Help me,
My confidence to gain,
I need someone to help me
See further than the rain.
Rebecca Ellen Godden

My Son
(*Dedicated to son, Michael Daniel*)

I look at you each day my son,
I watch you grow with pride,
You've filled the darkest place within,
Were sorrow once did hide.

A love I never knew could be,
Oh lord, you gave this gift to me,
A son to love forever more,
For I never knew this love before.

I love you more than words can say,
It's a love that grows day by day,
My son, you are the life in me,
and to my heart you hold the key.
Sheila Farrer

Visually Impaired Adoration
Following in your footsteps
With my bucket and spade,
Digging up the turf to take home and worship.
It is hardly a fit way to carry on.

I don't usually agree, on principle
With living icons,
But in your case
I'm prepared to make an exception.

A worthy investment in human nature,
You were somebody's energy well spent.
Your space, rent free from natural constraint.
You are everything that I perspire to be,
But sometimes sweat just isn't enough,
Blood and tears, they must be given as well.

This is the soft co-option.
Joining up the dots of our acquaintance
(If only in my mind).
I'm seeking to find . . .
Kevin Mitchell

Metamorphosis of the Mind

A metamorphosis of the mind,
releasing another kind.
Turning itself into something else.
From man to beast.

Lonely do I dwell,
in my own private hell.
Do I enjoy being here?
Getting constantly drunk,
on filthy beer.

Or have I passed on to another plain?
I cannot tell.
Time, that great observer,
looking through the glass darkly.
Into what?

I haven't a clue,
But now I have you.
My sweet love,
my future life,
my future wife.
My longing and waiting is now over.

Two hearts joined by love,
did it come from above?
No it came from just two,
me and you.

Now my mind is where it wants to be,
with you my love.
Not in the wilderness or the sea.
Me with you,
you with me.
Mike J P McManus

Free

I'm free of you,
No more soft lies,
No more pain,
No more cries in vain,
No more sorrows,
No more soft lies.

I'm free to smile,
I'm free to laugh,
I'm free to love,
At last I'm free of you,
I won't even think of you.
Deanne Lees

Old Age is Golden

Do you think old age is good?
Do you feel as well as you should?
Are your eyes as bright today?
As you thought they were yesterday?
What did you think when they gave you steak?
And found it was more than you could take.

A crusty roll you could not chew;
And to stand for long you cannot do.
When your glasses you lose once again;
You find you cannot even write your name.
You have arthritis and cannot walk,
Must be thankful that you can talk.

You go to bed, your teeth come out;
Also hearing aid you can't be without.
Your heart pumps faster - than you like it to do,
Slippers you wear, 'cause you can't get on your shoe.
Put in curlers to crimp your hair;
Should get up and go; but don't know where.

Life's hard, but must put on a brave grin,
And laugh to think of the state you're in.
Is this what they call the *Golden Age*?
If so I'd like to turn over the page.
Just a few prayers makes the world seem bright,
Then in the morning everything will be alright.

The sun will chase away the grey
And it truly will be a *Golden Day*.
K M Osborne

The Up and Down Days
I am a bus conductor
A dying race they say
I have to agree with them
I'm dying every day,
I feel like this when rising
From slumber that is deep
That clock's a ruddy nuisance
It seems to hate my sleep.
Anyway everybody's dying
From the day that they were born

Of course I'm no exception
So why should I be forlorn,
You see I'm near retirement
I can tell so, by me feet
So soon I'll take it easy
And rest and 'ave me sleep.
But will I be so tired
When I go to bed at night
And 'ave a proper shut eye
With muscles slack and slight,
Of course there's no foretelling
What hobbies I'll pursue
So watch out you young ladies
I might be after you!
E R Ferris

Old John

He stumbles along the busy street
His bones so creaky, his hands so chilly.
Where is he going, who will he see?
Oh, that loose step, misery me.

People pass by and glance at his frame
Poor old chap with glassy eyes.
Is he a tramp, or is he quite sane?
Leans on a wall, just a space, just a space.

Old John looks wearily to the flagged floor.
Pulls himself to and pushes afore.
There's a pint of the best, and then there is bed.
Rest, rest, rest.
Marian Sutcliffe

In Memory of a Friend

What did they say? 'Why be so upset,
he was *only a dog*' -
And life will be easier for you
now that he's gone.
No more hand trying to brush up the loose hairs,
That clung to the carpets, his chair, and the stairs,
You can now visit friends who live further away -
And stay out much longer, yes, even all day.
No bark will warn sea gulls to *get off your shed*,
Nextdoor's cats can scratch deeper in your flower beds.

The paint will stay cleaner inside the front door,
While no torn up paper scatters the floor.
You'll be much *better off* with no dog food to buy -
Of course, this is all true, then why should I cry?

Trees in a field had his daily attention,
Trained, not to soil streets, (and that's worth a mention),
Nor a long pedigree, just *first cross kind*,
And like many other friends, he had his own mind.
Ah! The bondage was mine, I was ever aware,
When I needed a friend, he was always there,
Through good days, and sad days of mixed emotion.
With eyes, (and his tail) showed me, unending devotion, -
So, I've moved, lead and collar from its well worn place, -
But - fifteen years love - would I want to erase?
I can only hope, that the heartache will go -
For my dear faithful, *Scampi*
I miss you so.
E M Seflon

Father's Day

Because this is your special day
I'd just like you to know
I love you very much dear dad
Though my feelings I don't always show

To me you are my hero dad
I'll always look up to you
Because you mean so much to me
In everything you do
I remember in my younger days
You'd sit me on your knee
You'd talk to me for hours dad
Those were special times for me
You'd take me out on day trips
To the park or to the zoo
You'd buy me sweets and ice-cream
Things mum said you shouldn't do
She'd always tell you off
But in a friendly sort of way
Because she knew you'd always spoil me
No matter what she had to say
I know you'll always love me dad
The same as I'll always love you
I know you'll always look after me
Although I've caused problems for you
So although I've grown older now
I'd still just like to say
I wish you love and happiness
Every minute of every day.
Susan Rogers

Friendship

What do you do when your heart aches?
When you're feeling full of despair
What do you do when you're lonely?
When you feel as if no one is there

How do you cope when you're feeling empty
and dead deep inside?
How can you carry on smiling,
When all you want - is to run and to hide?

What makes you carry on living
When you feel that you just can't go on?
How can you carry on giving,
When all that you do turns out wrong?

We all need people around us to love us
and to care
The way of coping with worthlessness
is to be honest, and our feelings to share.

What I'm trying to say to you dear friend
Is thankyou for standing by
And thankyou for that special gift -
A shoulder on which to cry.

You've listened to my problems and
tried to understand
Even when I've been selfish
You've been there to lend a hand.

There's one thing that I've learnt from life
We don't know what the future holds
We don't know what fate has in store for us -
Or if we'll even grow old.

But there's one thing that I'm certain of
If things get too much to bear
I will always be here for you
And I know you'll always be there.
A J Tucker

The Prestwick Hero

The night was cold and foggy
When the foreman gave a roar,
'The 'planes are all at Prestwick
And we're bound for that fair shore.'

To the cat he murmured softly,
And his voice was smooth as silk,
'Draw four mice from the store
And half a pint o' milk.'

We had to stop a Paisley,
Fro the fog had clamped right doon;
Outside the bus, a collie dog
Was running roon' and roon'.
'Grab him boys,' the foreman roared
In a voice that made us quail,
'Tie him to the front o' the bus
With a candle on his tail.'

The candlelight pierced the foggy night,
The dog gave joyous barks,
He couldn't wag his tail at all,
For all he had was sparks.
We'll never forget that terrible run
to Prestwick in the fog.
Marooned at Paisley and only saved
By the courage of a dog -

Later awarded the OBE
And four pats upon his back,
And where his tail once used to be,
He wags a Union Jack.
Walter McCorrisken

Who?

Who picks you up when you fall
      on your face
And dusts you down
      with a smile?
Then tells you to try
      and try again
For the effort will make it
      worthwhile

And sends you back into
      life's bitter brawl
With nothing to fight with
      but hope
Who ever he is, get rid
      of him quick
Or finish up punch drunk
      you dope.
Alan McIntosh

My First Day

It's seven o'clock,
Time to get up,
What's on today then?
School, arrgh!

I ate my breakfast,
Washed my face,
Put on my shoes,
Picked up my case.

I walked to my tutor,
All shining and new,
Oh! Where is it now?
Please give me a clue.

When I was at my tutor,
We played some games,
Of clapping and clicking,
All about names.

We went to the canteen,
To eat our food,
Some of the big boys,
Were being a bit rude.

I went to technology,
With Mrs Widlake,
I sewed up my fingers,
Oh! What a mistake.

The bell went,
Home time had come,
Pick up your bags,
And run, run, run.
Robert Down (11)

I Want to do This
I want to do this, I want to do that,
I want to do everything,
I want this and that.

I want to own a racecourse,
I would be a National owner,
But even that would make me lonelier.

I want to go in the space shuttle,
I want to go into space,
It would really be exciting to go
to another place.

But I still haven't got these things yet,
It will take a while to go,
But still it might be the same,
You never know.
Victoria E Parker (8)

The Passage of Time
Time keeps on drifting (drifting, drifting) into the future,
We have only memories to interpret the past;
Like beats on a drum, time moves rhythmically on,
And hints that our lives are running too fast.

Like clouds in the sky (moving, parting),
Stages in life become clear and are gone.
We understand nothing and experience everything,
And attempt to link it together as one.

Our thoughts are in flight (soaring, circling),
With the freedom to roam like a bird in the sky;
As subtle as night-time whispers in treetops,
Time and our dreams together collide.

To form a book of images, a lifetime of stories;
Silvery threads like cobwebs in dew,
Which link past with present and future with past
And the hearts of the people and the Me and the You.

The innocent minds of beautiful children,
Overfull with ideas and emotions which flow;
Our bodies which die as time passes by,
Yet our minds continue to flourish and grow.

Fed by the stimuli, our senses are nourished,
The vibrance of sound and brightness of colour;
The deepness of seas and the softness of waves;
The ticking of Time in the tongues of the fire.

Can Time understand or even empathise, with
The pain and the suffering passed down through centuries;
With the deep-furrowed brow and purple shadow of yes;
With our manger and remorse and petty jealousies?

Do the enchantment of innocence and enrichment of spirit
Really cushion our fall from the sureness of death?
Do the emotions of love and the warmth of the heart
Enable us to peacefully exhale our last breath?

Only Time will tell what we are to become,
What path we will take and what we seem to have done,
Where our minds will lead us, where our bodies will follow,
Only Time will know what will bring our *Tomorrow*.
Clare Juttner-Schmid

Empire Flying Boat
Cordelia southbound
Soliloquy to starboard

The day's flight now is nearly done
The light will soon fade fast
Tomorrow night real rest at last!
More rest, then maybe fun!

The float stays draw their pencilled lines
Criss cross the sunset's blaze
The floats are little boats themselves
Hanging in the haze

Pegasus and Pegasus!
To port the twins again
Beatibg, always beating
Through cloud, silk mist, or rain

The snowmen shuffle across the sky
Like human aged men
Their billowed folds have grown all day
Nimbus now, then dew again!

Cordelia! I feel drowsy
And soon I'll be asleep
Wake me up at Lumbo
Banking hard and steep.
Ward Gray

The Prisoner

Beyond my shuttered eyes I know the sky is blue
And the fields and forests meet in shades of green,
And there are loving faces, blurred beyond recall
And other, younger faces I have never seen.

But colours are just words to tease the mind
Where light and shade are only flickering rays,
And all the beauty of the outside world
Is stolen by the dark of night-time days.

I was not born a prisoner, I was free,
As a child I saw the images you know,
But blindness closed my eyes upon the scene
And shut the gates of freedom long ago.

I know the fields are still of shimmering green
And wisps of snow-white paint the cloudy skies,
But the beauty I knew once and which is lost
In colours now is echoed through *your* eyes.
Ann Rutherford

The Curtain

Black is my colour
it hangs like a drape
I'm closing my eyes
so the tears can't escape.

Why am I such?
this used not to be
Like a curtain drawn over
I can no longer see.

It's as if my small world
has splintered and shattered
I dwell on such things
that once never mattered.

In my ideal world
there would always be
Two strong loving arms
to hold onto me.

Someone who would help me
to regain my place
I just want to take part
in the human race.
Carolyne Calder

Untitled

Experience counts for nothing
Of that you can be sure
It's only when your on the *dole*
A disease without a cure.

You feel your on the scrap-heap
And nothing's going right
The future, if there is one
Doesn't look too bright.

I pray a job will come along
To give my life a lift
Up at dawn - and off to work
It would truly be a gift.
John Miller

Desire

As the wind blows the tassels of her silken hair
her thoughts tormented in the silent hour.
Little does she know the love she feels
will leave her all alone on Winter's hill.

Another time, another place, another dream
all she wanted, could have been.
But alas, poor maiden, ice queen too
sorrow has cast its shadow over you.

Doomed to be trapped in mind alone
as to another, he is prone.
Intangible, internal tomb of desire
erupt, external, extinguish the fire.
Mary Carradice

Memory

Is this the road we walked in childhood days
Between the fields of corn and dappled copse,
Where humming insects filled the summer air
And birds, swift-flying, swooped from tree to tree,
Or sunbeams slanted on the frost-rimed fields
And rooks cawed sadly o'er the furrowed land?
Is this straight length of stone-curbed concrete way
The dusty lane we tramped along to school,
Chasing bright butterflies upon the verge?

Across the bridge there stood old Reubin's house
Half buried in the trees and ivy-clad,
Which we would dare each other to approach
With mingled fear and pleasure in the deed.
Beyond the house there ran a tumbling stream
Which crossed the lane at Micklebury Ford
And hurried on between the distant hills
To find its way at last into the sea.

And further on there stood the village school,
Its harshness softened by the passing years,
My memory recalls its happy times.
And after school we played in Horley Woods
And climbed the trees, picked bluebells in the spring
And gathered blackberries in the autumn days.

Now house and woods and school are swept away
Another generation walks this road.
I thought to turn the clock back to my youth
And see the old familiar scene again.
Alas, it is no more but I give thanks
I knew it once and still the memory lives
In a quiet secret recess of my mind.
Heather Brackley

Remembrance

Here, in the quietness under the moon
Thy presence is lingering yet.
Here, 'neath the dewy-dip't branches of June
Thy sweetness I cannot forget.

Down in this garden of mystical charms
We kissed, and the nightingales knew
While you were sheltering close in my arms,
The spring of their lilting was - You!
Eric G Williams

People of the Black Country

The nicest folk are Black Country folk
People who'll *help out* at times,
When you're in *dire straits*
When you've upset your mates
Well, anything along these lines.
They're *always there with a helping hand,*
Now'ts too much trouble, 'tis true.
When you're in a mess,
Your girl wouldn't say *yes*
Black Country folk are for you.

They don't make a fuss, big-hearted they come,
They work incognito - what's more,
A welcome is ready, willing hands too
When you need help to knock at their door,
You're invited inside, made comfy, served tea,
There's nothing they want in return
But to be unselfish like Black Country folk
Is a lesson we'll all have to learn.
Betty Lake

Jeans, Jeans, Jeans, Jeans . . .

Blue jeans, black jeans, grey and green,
All were part of the sixty's scene.
Ever hanging lifeless on the line
Waiting for young men in their prime.

Hot days, cold days, windy and wet,
Hanging, dripping, waiting the *Jet Set.*
Mothers cursing as they banged the iron
Mourning the passing of suits with tie on.

Fat lads, slim lads, young and teens,
All chameleons when in their jeans
Hair sleeked back and Elvis pose
Walk the streets and sing their woes.

Fat girls, slim girls, young and silly
Eye the lads and dream of Billy,
Pouting lips and strutting jeans
This, they dreamed, is what life means!

Weekdays, holidays, birthdays and Lent
Washing jeans was how days were spent.
Cardboard cut-outs curses mothers,
Whilst ironing jeans for sons and brothers.

Seventies, eighties, now nineties as well,
Who'd have thought they would still be a sell?
How many million have been cursed and patched?
How many million have been loved and matched?

New jeans, old jeans, darned and faded
Still going strong, though the bodies are jaded.
Mothers' from the sixties fading like the jeans
Still spare a thought for the next kings and queens.
Bronwyn Terry

Memories of Blackpool

My memories of Blackpool go back a long way.
When mum and dad took us all there for the day.
My four sisters and I, 'twas a rare treat for sure.
For in that day and age, we were all very poor.

We set off from Church, a small place in East *Lanky*.
On the train, with our buckets and spades and clean hanky,
Through Rishton and Blackburn, and stations galore,
Till at last we reached Blackpool, and made for the shore.

Mum had packed up our *butties*, it was cheaper you see,
Than paying for seven, in a café for tea.
But to sit and enjoy them, in the lovely fresh air
Was delightful, and then we all went on the fair.

We all had one ride on whatever we picked,
While mum and dad watched us - and then we all licked
Delicious ice cream, just a small one, that's all.
And then we all played on the beach, with a ball.

We built a sandcastle all stately and trim,
With a moat that filled with water when the tide came back in.
Then off to watch rock being made different hues.
And dad bought some, lettered with *Blackpool* right through.

Then off to the train, that took us back home,
After a wonderful day, filled with laughter and fun.
I can still hear the seagulls flying over the sea,
On our once a year outing, now a sweet memory.
Olive Smith

So Much Love
I have loved you
So much
Much more
Than most,
But I cannot
Love you
Much more
Than I do.
I have stood
At your side
Night after night
Day after day,
As the year
Goes by
I have been there
For your children,
As well as
Your sickness
As well
As your health;
But you still
Expect more
But I cannot love
You more
Than I already do.
Tracy Salt

Today, Tomorrow and Yesterday
Tear stained faces push open doors, doors which lead to
the despair of today, the heartbreak of yesterday and the
consequence of tomorrow.

Today will be tomorrow's yesterday, filled with the wish
that humanity had been kind, love had won over truth.

Yesterday holds the heartbreak of dreams, heartbreak of
memories that punish our every move from our tired limbs.
Dreams of tomorrow that seemed sweet yesterday have
turned into the bitter reality of today.

Tomorrow stands holding the key to unlock the
yesterdays and todays of the tomorrows yet to come. Do we
take the key and unlock our hearts to pour out the bad or
keep it in until it becomes a dark and stagnant desire to
wage war and hate which is shown in all mortal minds. The
other keys have been twisted so they no longer fit the
lock, tomorrow's is shining and new, it holds the promise
we long for.

Do we take it before it becomes tarnished like
yesterday and today? We can mould the lock to fit the
key, the key which holds our future, tomorrows and
yesterdays.
Helen King

Where Has the Time all Gone
It started in the forty's,
When I came upon the scene,
The fifty's were my schooldays,
I was never very keen,
The sixty's they were swinging
I really had some fun.

97

I also had four babies
That kept me on the run,
The seventy's they were mad days,
Rushing kids from here to there,
Always in my platforms,
And my latest pair of flares,
The eighty's were my favourite,
The kids with all their mates,
Drinking cups of coffee
Watching videos till late.
Now we're in the ninety's
The kids have all left home,
They now have homes and families
And problems of their own.
A new century will soon be here
We know it won't be long,
And I sometimes sit and wonder,
Where has the time all gone?
D Sharpe

After The Land-Mine 1941

A sea of roofs apon the ground,
Tinkling glass and the intermidable sweeping,
Dust still rising, leaden skies,
But then, I saw no weeping.

We stood and stared,
'It missed our park, but look, that's where our Co-op was',
'And that,' said you (with half a smile remembering the hours of dark)
'Was where I was awhile.'

Then I recalled the dark night hours,
While sheltering there beneath the ground,
We'd heard your heavy booted tread,
Approaching down the garden path, an unfamiliar sound.

We'd feared the enemy had come,
And listened there, with bated breath,
Until we heard your voice,
Relief and joy then knew no bounds.

We listened while you told your tale,
Eyes shining in the candlelight,
The long trek home,
While bombs rained down, and you were all alone.

Journey almost at an end,
The land-mine came down with blast and roar,
Unscathed, you turned and walked back to
This scene of havoc and bad dreams.

So now, we stood and looked again,
'How close' (we thought) but did not say,
I looked at you, you held my hand,
We sighed, and sadly turned away.
Elsie Phillips

Don't Turn Away
My arms yearn to hold you,
Just hear what I say,
I love you, my darling,
And want you to stay,
Please don't turn away,
There's no-one quite like you,
So don't make me pay.

Oh, my heart is breaking,
Because I love you so,
So don't turn away,
Say that you love me,
That you will be mine,
Hold me tight and kiss me,
Just don't turn away.
Albert W J Knee

True Love

When I just saw you
I knew in my heart
That I'd love you
And we'd never part.

I wanted our life
To be shared together
I didn't know then
It wouldn't last for ever.

For God took you from me
And I mourn your going
For now I can't see you
Anymore without knowing.

Did you love me
As I loved you?
Was it a dream
Or really true?

Was it yesterday?
Or was it last week?
When you held my hand
And you kissed my cheek?

Time passes
And the days slip by
Was it yesterday
You wiped
The tear from my eye?

Sleep my love
Until eternity
And I'll be with you
When God sets me free.
Joy Cosaitis

Love

The carrier of passions
Ardency arising,
Under a hammer
Behind the anvil,
A loves dues
Are fragmented.

The friends mark
A gentle reminder,
Of a surrendered piety
Is touched by halves.

Light spirits awakened
For a loves adornment,
Once felt
Forever assimilated.

Love dawns interestingly
Frequented internally,
Whispers in parting
Naturally
Step by step.
Alan Trussell

Lost Love

Green quiet hills where I first met my love
Sheep in the grass, the blue sky above,
Rose in her cheeks, her eyes all aglow,
Hills of my youth, and the sea below.

Green quiet hills, she is gone, she is gone
Sheep in the byre the mist lingers on,
Pale were her cheeks, her eyes full of woe
Hills of my age and the sea below.
P Melville Richards

His Love for Me

I always ask him at the break of day,
Please help me Lord upon my way,
To join me Lord,
In what I have planned,
You bring so much joy and pleasure to me,
Peace and contentment for all to see,
I turn to you Lord in trouble and strife,
And to share with you of the joys and beauties of life,
And last thing at night,
As I close my eyes,
I say my prayers without any fears.
I love you Lord and I know you love me,
When I'm weary Lord come to me,
Let me be found in your loving clasp,
For eternal life, I wish at last.
Rosemary Curtis

Untitled

To feel your body close to mine,
Arms around you,
Legs entwined.
Lips meet to kiss, and then
With two hearts that beat as one.
Hands caress and this is when
The web of love for you is spun.
Lips that kiss and tongue that tease,
Mounting passion has begun.
Hands and fingers there to please,
Two bodies joining into one.
As we cuddle close, holding tight
A fairy kiss brushes a cheek.
Love is a blanket for the night
Together now we fall asleep.
Julie Hunt

Day Dreams

If I could find a new love
With whom to share my life
I could then be someone's mistress
Instead of mother and wife.

Although I love my husband
And my children are just great
It would really be exciting
Just to stay out very late.

Instead of cooking and washing
And housework all day long
I could lounge upon the sofa
And listen to his song.

My day dreaming days are over
I'm far too old to care
I've got a happy marriage
But I could do with an au-pair.
Janet Davis

The Gift

I am grown tired of loving you,
Your heart is cold, 'tho once I thought 'twas mine.
Your eyes, which should be mirrors of your soul,
Are bleak, and no light from them shine.
- And yet, and yet, so lustily you live,
But warmth, and tenderness, these you cannot give.
And as flowers need the sun to grow
Will wilt and die, when left to face the snow,
So does my heart need kindness and love
Not hidden by dark clouds from above.

Perhaps there's someone on your mind to whom you could
Be loving, kind, and true
- I shall not know,
The Gods have had their fun,
They gave me you,
And so, to them I'll pay my due
I'll give them back the gift they gave.
Maybe, someday you will recall
The one who gladly gave you all
And asked for nothing - save a kiss.
- Then found you could not grant me this . . .
Dorothy Page

Once Again

When I am with you
It's as if I am dreaming
Knowing not how it really started
Of how it will ever end.
Will I awaken too soon?
What if I awaken too late?
Can love really be so great?
Playing along with the game
Not knowing if I will ever win.
Am I dreaming?
Can things be so good?
Can love be true?
If I awaken
Will reality come to an end?
If I am dreaming
I would rather dream
Than be heart broken
Once again!
M Bond

Love Never Dies
He stood where they had stood only
A year ago,
Listening to the carols,
Watching falling snow
They had gone into the church and
Favourite carols sung,
Why had God taken her,
So beautiful, so young?
He raised his hands to heaven,
Knowing she was there,
Shutting out all other thoughts,
And said this simple prayer,
'If I could have but one wish,
It would be to be with you,
To share your life in every way,
In everything you do,
To have love and joy, and laughter,
Every moment of each day,
True love in the hereafter,
Which now seems so far away,
But one day I know my life will end,
As every life must do,
And when it does, my sweetheart,
My life will be with you.'
Barrie Strong

Love is
Love is so much like a rose
It opens so slowly, so sweetly
Until its bloom is full of life
Then its vein is cut
The bloom is shed,
The flowers dead
Leaving painful memories ahead.
Barry Challen

Now We Move on

My life is over, my love is lost, but I'm forced to live this lie
For this man is my friend and he doesn't yet know that it's time
          to say goodbye,
I have seen the signs and read them well and this game that
          we play's not the same
Where once we would give only counsel and love, we seek only
          to punish and blame.
It is I who's at fault, for he follows my rules, where once I would
          strike and he'd wince
His eyes that were once filled with love now go cold, he strikes
          back, with not even a flinch,
All the time we are hurting each other more deepiy, drifting ever
          more slowly apart
He not even aware, I only half conscious, that we both destroy
          each others heart.
Everyday I cry out, please listen to me, share with me some of
          your thoughts
Each night I lay listening wrapped in his arms, to silence, I feel
          so distraught,
I act so irrational when he states he has friends that he really
          would like to see
I think of him talking and laughing with them, when a stranger
          he is out with me.
But his need for me's less, he's moved on I can see, I can't bind
          him to me as I try
To pretend that our union's a union of souls is no less I have
          learnt than a lie,
And though I am left with my dream all aruin, I know now that
          my anger's unjust
For it's me now that needs to move on and grow, to survive I
          am certain I must.
If we part now as friends, in time we'll look back and deep in
          our hearts we will know
That the love we have shared, has now been saved, for truly
          loving is letting go.

Melody Wood

Untitled

I need you, so help me,
When dreams torment me, and cynics dement me
And deceit prevails in reasons beyond me.
When my mind turns to folly with the wine that I drink
And my thoughts, when they scare me.

I need you, rehearse me
In the parts I should play when I am without you,
The thoughts I should say when I am with you,
When people are laughing and I don't know why
And my words, when they choke me.

I love you, so guide me,
As I stumble deeper through darkness,
With black clouds rolling over my head.
When my heart is breaking and my body is aching
And my dreams all seem to be dead.

And I love you, console me
In times of despair and my insecurities
Just be there, to hold me.
Janice Williams

Snowy Feelings

That time has come when things are done
And now we're both alone
You're going your way-out of mine
You're free and your own.
The ground is white, I sit and stare
Of snow just falling down
Small thin flakes lie on my hand
So gentle, so light, no sound
Even though our hope we had
Just drifted far apart

It seems that snow has found a way
Of reaching in my heart
The hurt of all inside of me
Of thinking how you look
I hope that you will not forget
The feelings that you took
The snow has settled here to stay
It will not be for long
As long as I still think of you
Till out my heart you're gone
Lonely I feel without you near
Still see that in the snow
A little space apon the ground
My tears have made a flow
My thoughts and tears have gathered
They knew that I had part
They formed a lonely figure
Of a sad and broken heart
Peter A Spendlove

The Woman in Nineteen Twenty
The woman in Nineteen Twenty
Has a most annoying habit
Of letting her thoughts drift away
Across the quagmire of the years
To me and I don't like it.
The pain in her life is not my affair,
Her wishes for the future only sadden my heart
To share her existence
Does not end loneliness
It merely softens the edges.

I stand outside her head and watch
Although I should be somewhere else
Doing something useful.
She lassos my legs with her thoughts
And I say, 'Yes'
As she searches for something lasting
That reaches beyond Nineteen Twenty
And I say, 'I've seen it all before'
She just laughs in my brain
And carries on looking
For a find to shake my cynicism -
Unusual,
This particular woman
In this particular Nineteen Twenty.
Eddie Malone

Autumnal Love?

In the cold night air of winter
We kissed
From the steam of our breath
You sculptured a heart
From what I thought was stone.

Together we thawed
Holding on to
Each other we bloomed
Petals, opened out, revealing
Colours
Skin to skin, I cherished your voice
Your touch
You were my flower, fragile.

In the summer sun we reclined
Into each others souls
Discovering secrets, we shared a body, a mind
We were comfortable and content
Basking in love, resplendent.

Now I gaze
At you at your most beautiful
In the autumnal shades
Holding on to
The memories
And the fears, that we may grow apart
Cold,
That the golden leaves
Will fall.
Richard Wadman

My Sailor

I stood on the dockside dressed in black,
You looked at me and I looked back,
The look of love my heart did say,
Then you quickly sailed away,
You sailed away to another land,
Where you took another hand,
Then you came back as before,
Where I was waiting by the shore,
We strolled off hand in hand,
And talked about the other lands.
Phyllis Newman

Memory Lane

Wild winds dance, the skies acclaim,
thrashing raindrops against my window pane.
How comforting is home, where the wood stove glows,
seated and warmed, from the kisses it throws.
When the mind meanders so aimlessly,
down little lanes of our memory.
Come for a stroll! Right to my heart,
down a little lane, that I'll ne'er depart.

Ah! Emerald green a colour maybe,
or painted island surrounded by sea.
Serene in beauty so gentle it's ways,
a distant mirage of Irish days.
Steeped deep in history, their lands do hold,
preserved, *mastered* from fathers of old.
Mountains, lakes, forests of pine,
sweet breath of air, pure and fine.
Rugged walls of cobbled stone,
little white cottage - a home to home.
A smiling greet of sincerity,
with open hands and generosity.
Irish hearts that love to give,
who'll sing, joke, take time and live.
Bless you now! This I pray,
tomorrow will bring a peaceful day.
In memory or dreams anything can be,
true harshness of life, is its reality.
I wander back from my little lane,
where wild winds dance in the pouring rain.
Mandy A McLaren

Memories of Childhood

I long to find a bluebell wood
  Seek bluebell growing wild
To walk those leafy lanes again
  Pick bluebells as a child,
To make again a daisy chain
  My flowered dress, to grace
Believe again, that fairies dwell
  And hide in that secret place.
Once more, to see a spiders web
  Woven on a hawthorn bough
With rays of sunshine, dancing
  To sparkle and endow,

To sit beside a lively stream
  And watch with eager eyes
To see the tiny fishes, dart
  And chase those dragonflies.
If I could be a child again
  Return to days of yore
I would find again sweet happiness,
  In bluebell woods, once more.
Olive Muir

As I Remember

For he once stood there in glory and pride'
  But now alone . . . he sits . . . looking neglected denied.
His roof slipping slates so they're bearing all'
  To above open skies . . . from where the patter of rain does fall.
Cast iron gutters torn from where it clung to its Eaves'
  So hanging helpless . . . simply collecting falling leaves.
The pebbledash walls once carefully painted white'
  Now . . . crack . . . split . . . subside from morning till night.
Once where one peered from windows of lead'
  The wood now to rotten . . . to hold them in bed.
An old heavy oak door still guards its way'
  From unwelcome guests . . . unwanted prey.
Through in a hall a staircase did stand'
  For there in a corner . . . once a clock tocked grand.
Stone sink in the kitchen where a tap drops a drip'
  The larder now bare . . . not a morsel nor pip.
Grand was the fire whom spat sparks at its hearth'
  Bellowing smoke up its chimney . . . keeping out any draft.
A bed lie resting laid out in a heap'
  For where the farmer and wife . . . in the bedroom . . . would sleep.
What became of all the land that surround'
  The barns and stables . . . not a nah, not a sound.
For where is the orchard the lane that pass through'
  Now since long gone . . . if then . . . if only we knew.
Stands now all homes for those of old age'
  It said life must go onward . . . so to turn another page.
Mark J Clarke

Memories

The night is still, and vigil lone I keep,
The stars and I together, while around me sleep
My comrades, spent with weariness and strain,
That all too soon the grey of dawn will bring again;
My thoughts take wing, to swiftly homeward fly,
And time is not, nor space, as gently passing by
Each vision brings a memory that stays forever green,
And now unfolds within my heart, to bridge the years between.
I hear once more the friendly creak of swinging garden gate,
And see the open door, where smiling loved ones wait,
I feel their tender, warm caress, the thrill of happy pride,
The joy of coming home again at quiet eventide
I see a tiny night-gowned form, head bowed in lisping prayer,
And hear the sound of baby feet, upon the winding stair.
I listen to a lullaby, as on a mother's breast
Sleepy little eyelids close in childhood's perfect rest
I feel the warmth and comfort of an old familiar room,
With curtains drawn as daylight fades, before the winter's gloom
While in the firelight's flickering glow, the shadows on the wall
Dance in silent rhythm, as the embers gently fall.
The clock upon the mantel shelf ticks on its merry way,
And children's happy voices echo faintly from their play.
Amid its lazy, wispy steam, the kettle softly sings,
And all around me, dwells the peace of simple homely things.
I sigh, and as the visions fade, once more I stand alone,
A thousand miles away from all the happiness I've known.
Yet even in the loneliness and longing of my heart,
I feel the precious warmth that golden memories impart -
Till somewhere down the road of time, with Armageddon past,
My cherished memories and I, shall meet again at last.
William Spalding

Victorian Times

My granny reminisces Victorian days
Cobbled streets and alleyways.
Smoky mills and smoggy skies
Starch collars, thin dark ties.
The pilfering urchin on the street
Holes in breeches and nowt on his feet.
'There's a penny lad for some cake'
A cheeky face the scamp would make.
Those pennyfarthing bikes and
Flat capped men and braces
Tough boots with ropy laces.
Poverty, hard times, values set
Rules were firm and always met.
There was also a fair bit of
Wealth in those days
Big fat wallets and the worker pays.
On a Sunday you wore your best
Granddad by the hearth in longjohns and vest.
Dainty shops with sweeties in jars
Liquorice sticks and candy bars.
Oh how I'd love those merry days
The boy in the street with marbles he plays.
Gathering around the piano singing songs
And me - my heart just longs and longs.
Strict and fair my granddad would be
Not a nicer chap you'd see.
He'd work at the mill and granny would bake.
Soda bread and almond cake.
I'd love the Victorian era if only for a day
And I bet you a farthing I'd long and long to stay.
Janet Riley

Will They all Fade Away With the Passing of Time

Thinking aback when I was ever so small,
Tales told to me that now seem ever so tall,
Warnings handed down by some very old wife,
Sometimes have directed the path of my life

Remember 'tis bad luck the spilling of salt,
What one must do to remedy this fault,
Before you age and grow one minute older,
Throw small pinch of salt, over your left shoulder

Take heed, do not walk under that leaning ladder,
Less kith and kin become so much the sadder,
Suffer not a kiss from the angel of death,
Nor embrace of the rope that robs one of breath

Come, run away children from that lucious green pool,
So inviting to small ones the water's so cool,
Jinny will catch you with her large green teeth,
You'll be lost forever in the waters beneath

April Noddy is with us, the day of the cod,
Armed with pencil and paper, please give us a nod,
Twelve noon it's all over, Noddy's past and gone,
Don't be branded a Noddy with thinking it's still on

A break for old housewives round table they sup,
Eagerly waiting fro that last twirl of the cup,
Upside down is the cup, then the reading of leaf,
Some may doubt teller, but for others it's belief

Encourage him not this old bird of woe,
Hand in hand is misfortune with wily old crow,
Upon ones house he must never be let stay,
Unwelcome he is, you must chase him away

Pancake Tuesday, man and maid takes a turn,
The tossing of pancakes for fear they may burn,
The day upon when both rich and the poor,
Every stomach is filled and can hold nothing more

Customs and beliefs from time long ago,
Some are forgotten, some you may know,
Rekindled in memory in this my fond rhyme,
Will they all fade away with the passing of time.
Frank Bamber

Sounds of the Past

I loved the sound of horses feet,
Echoing, on the cobbled street,
The milk float, the little old man
Ladles and jugs, and clattering cans.

Lying in bed I would hear a cock crow,
A whistling collier, on way to work would go,
Mill girls laughter, in the morning air,
Hurrying by, not a moment to spare.

In the air a smell of fog, in the distance the morning train,
Clitter clatter, the sound of clogs, time you were getting up again,
Pitter patter, sound of rain, swishing on the window pane,
Out of bed, slippers on, wishing you could get back again.

Kettle singing on the hob, cat meowing at the door,
Post man comes, letters he drops, then comes the singing paper
boy,
At the top of the street, a coal merchant arrives,
Telling his wares. *Coal* he cries.

Rag a bone man, in the back street,
His singing lament, was a rare treat,
A balloon for a jam jar, donkey stone for rag,
But nothing for old bones in a bag.

And when the day is over, and I try to sleep,
The worst of all the noises is when someone starts to snore,
And when I finally find sleep, in the middle of a dream,
the cock will suddenly crow, and wake me up once more.
Mary Seddon

116

I Remember
(*In memory of Ernest Sheppard 17.7.1912 - 28.11.1991*)

So far away,
On clouded memories that fade with time,
Ghostly faces haunt my distant past.

Families torn.
Time walked away, leaving emptiness
In a once innocent, happy boy.

Silvery droplets cried through flames of pain,
Dried with love which was needed so greatly.

Reunion of parted kin.
Gladness flowed from
Reddened eyes.

Yet one slipped through
Life's vast safe net.

No laughter shall I share,
And no jokes to tell.
No merry drunkenness
With his favourite beer.
Only a cold stone
Which bears his name.

I remember him
In one delicate memory
More precious than gold.
A mental photo
Which I cannot touch.

So my sorrow lingers
And time walks on.
But I will always remember
The one that slipped through.
The man they called
Grandad.
Paul Howard

Untitled

The stream tomorrow won't be so dank,
With lifeless mist that fills its bank,
No falling leaf into that mist,
Tomorrow's stream will be sunkissed,
Today's stream skulks past under shrouds,
Tomorrow's sky will have no clouds,
When the clock has turned its face,
We will see the stream in all its grace,
Darting silver, pebbles bright,
What a change over night,
Gurgles will reveal their source,
A kingfisher will flash along its course,
Tomorrow's stream won't hide in mist,
Tomorrow's stream will be sunkissed.
George Smith

A Friday Friend

Why aren't you my friend, then?
Why aren't you talking to me?
You were friends with me yesterday when
I had my pocket money.
We went to the fair. I paid for the rides,
All the ones you said you wanted.
We screamed with fright and cried with delight
At the train that was really haunted.

118

So why aren't you my friend anymore?
Why are you ignoring me?
I bet you'll be friends with me on Friday again,
When I get my pocket money.
Josephine Burnett

Time Passing

I would like to turn the clock back, to the time
                    when I was five,
To the day that I first started school, and my brain
                    became alive,
A whole new world opened up to me as I learned
                    to read and write
That was easy, but arithmetic, didn't always turn
                    out right.
With a ha'penny tied in the corner of a hanky
                    pinned to my slip,
to pay for the cocoa at playtime, so hot that
                    it burned by lip.
No free milk in 1931, hence the ha'penny for
                    the drink.
Made with water, and very strong, turned our
                    cheeks to a rosy pink.

I wouldn't turn the clock back, when I reached
                    my thirteenth year,
The second world war had just begun, and
                    our hearts were filled with fear,
We laughed in the face of adversity, cried
                    into our pillows at night.
As the boys with whom we'd gone to school,
                    were all called up to fight.
No more joy, and childish games, as the war
                    rolled on and on.
Some were shot from the sky in flames, others
                    killed by the bullet and bomb.

119

I will draw a veil on the years between,
                     till the boys who were left came back.
Never to tell how bad things had been, at
                     the times they were facing attack.

I married a soldier, returned in one piece,
                     except for the memories of war.
Hoping in future, that conflict would cease, and
                     peace would reign evermore.
A futile dream, for the world's in a mess, nothing
                     but trouble and strife.
Humanity suffers, I feel their distress as they
                     struggle to hang on to life.
We have old fashioned values, founded on faith,
                     which perhaps, some people might mock.
Things may get better as time passes by,
                     then we won't want to turn back the clock.

Iris Tromans

Memory

'Do you remember Elsie Beddoes who used to live at No. 23?'
She asked as I took in her piece of cake and afternoon cup of tea.
The central heating is on full blast and two bars of the electric fire
And there is a blanket over her legs and a closed book on her knee.

Casting my mind over the street where we have lived for thirty years
I try to recall all the neighbours who have been and gone,
'No,' I say, 'Who was she?'
'You must do - fair haired, stout, had two children or was it three?
She was always in an out at one time, funny, made you laugh
Her husband was with your father in the ARP.'
Which supplies the clue that it is fifty years ago she is thinking of
The war time years, living in the city.

She insists. Remembers them all from that long time ago, so clearly,
But cannot recall what you told her yesterday, so pacifying her
To avoid an upset, I pretend to agree.
But she shakes her head impatiently . . .

My son comes in and she tells him curiously
That I don't remember Elsie Beddoes, or her children,
She questions him, 'Does he?'
'You played with her children,' she tells him and he tries hard
To think back to the neighbours of his youth, but unsuccessfully.
'It was before he was born' I tell her, 'it must have been my brother'

But she won't have it. She can remember it so well, you see.
Can see them all now, those faces. They've come back to her again.
Sitting here in her chair, now she is ninety-three,
And Elsie Beddoes has survived in our peculiar conversation
My mother, out of the blue, has remembered her laughter
And Elsie Beddoes has achieved a strange immortality.
Beryl Ward

Yesterday
An old deep hurt can throb with unexpected pain,
Touched off by a careless chance remark.
The memory stirs to surface once again
From it's long buried and subconscious dark,
And going right back unto that former day,
For a fleeting moment time stands still,
Recalling that all was shattered,
And only grief did fill
The mind and heart.
No ray of hope to dull despair, or ease the way,
But life and time moves on,
It all was yesterday.
Marjorie Alix

dearest
   the sight of this being
         turns a normally placid person
   into a raging psychopath
  someone who can control themself ordinarily
 is thrown into violent overdrive
     rational, calm, thought dissipates.
  emotion overrides reason
      the anger builds, frustration . . .
              explodes . . .
    the knife lays dripping with
  the blood of the *enemy*,
     the enemy is dying on the floor.
 the *victim* sits in a corner
    unsure of the last few minutes
 the victim is the attacker,
     'didn't mean to hurt you mum' then
   'i only wanted you to hear me'
              She's dead . . .
 what was an argument because a murder
 two people who love each other also
                 hate each other,
 too much anger, led to tears . . .
      Be careful
           where you tread,
   the traps are there,
             inside your head.
Jessica Wright

Lend Me Your Ear
Lend me your ear
While I whisper
I don't want to tell you my fears
I just want to start reminiscing
Of happy times over the years

It doesn't take long to remember
The kids down our street that we knew
I remember all of their faces
Do you remember their names
'Yes I do.'

I can only remember the laughter
Of the mams when we did something mad
Yes I only remember the mothers
We didn't see much of the dads.

Everyone gathered together
At certain times of the year
Not only for funerals and weddings
Any excuse for a good cheer.

Do you remember the year the war started
And our mams said you don't have to fear
They're too far over the ocean
They'll never never get here
They rushed us down in the shelters
To try and sleep if we could
But we only wanted to listen
To the roar of the planes up above.

'Now' everyone's scattered all over
Some even over the sea
And I wonder if ever
When I think of them
If they ever think of me.
Mary Woodhead

Child's Play
Have the children of today
Lost the special gift of play?
What happened to *Skilly* our fun?
British Bulldog, Knock 'n' run?

123

'Jack, Jack shine a light' we would scream
but their fun's a computer screen.
Skipping ropes, whip 'n' top,
Hop scotch, we played the lot!
Popping tar, Ball 'n' Jacks
fish for Taddys, stickle backs.
They've Turtles, wrestlers, toys galore
within an hour 'Mum they're a bore!'
At school it's transformers in the yard
Who can swap a football card
We let our kids carry on our name
Why can't they carry on the game?
Have the children of today,
Lost the special gift of play?
L K Roscoe

The Drinker

I got home at 12.30
I'd been down to the pub
I'd had eight pints of bitter
Perhaps more than I should.

I'd had a hot pork sandwich
And a natter to my mates,
I'd chatted up the barmaid
And now my stomach aches.

If only I had got the sense
To know I'd had enough
And when I've had a social drink
Well then I'd just sup up.

I'd come home at an early hour
And go to bed quite snug
I'd wake up in the morning fit
And not feel I'd been mugged.

I've sworn I'll give it up before
I don't suppose I will
Tomorrow I'll be there again
I know I shall . . . I will . . .
Ron Smith

Farewell to a Cinema
Goodbye old friend, they have laid you to rest,
No longer the pleasure you gave us as we enjoyed your darkness,
We, simple we, revelled in fantasy in good days and in times
of stress.

Gone are those days, when young, we met our lovers and friends
Which gave us much happiness.
In the gloom we entered another world of action, fun and tears,
Held hands, smoked our smokes, which dissolved our fears,
Remember as kids on Saturday we sang our club song,
Good citizens when we grow up and champions of the free!

Thank you Roy Rogers, Randolph Scott, Buck Jones and
Gene Autry,
Thanks again for movietone news, Bogart, Cagney and serials
That kept us in our seat,
We are older now but still enjoyed the newcomers, Gibson,
Cruise and Streep
Soon your old frame will disintegrate from ball, hammer and
bulldozers
But the memory remains and always will, of better days from
we the picturegoers!
Robin S Cope

My Pet Hates
Supermarket queues, when my items are few,
Someone in front of me, with credit card too.
No chairs to sit on to rest your legs,
I'm going dizzy finding the eggs,
My trolley wheels won't go straight,
I'm really getting in a state.

I've searched around up every aisle,
I must have travelled over a mile.
I'll be able to enter the Marathon in May,
With all the training I've got in today!
At last I've finished and out of the store,
Don't think I'll shop here any more,
Now I've had my little moan,
I'll get the bus and make for home,
Have a cup of tea and a biscuit or two,
If I can open the packet (are they stuck with superglue?)
V Brough

Comfort

Lightening flashes singed the air,
Winds tore the clouds asunder.
Noise and tumult everywhere
With echoes of the thunder.
Sheets of rain clothed all the land,
The elements were wild.
Yet even nature hadn't planned
That deep inside its gloom,
Within a cottage room,
Was peace.
A mother with her child.
S G O Cook

The Tides of Time

So now I've decided that I'm growing old
Looking back from the mirror the story is told
I've ploughed my own furrow, time's softened my bark
Now only past scenes, rising flames in the dark.
But life's what you make it and I've played the game
Though time allocated, neither fortune or fame

I'm not complaining, 'cause I've reaped my reward
From love, good health, family and I thank the Lord,
The syndrome of realisation hangs heavy over me
Like most fools I'm blinkered, and don't want to see
But time takes its toll when you're young at heart
Wrinkles, blotches, feeble bones, play a minor part.
Ah! if on the other hand, I had the power to see
What's out there? who knows what's in store for me
Sure I'd cut my losses, sit back and be content
With the love I've had, a whole life well spent,
But its courage I need now that I'm growing old
When to eat, sleep and play, I don't want to be told
Senior citizen, maybe, don't class me second rate
Or cast me one side, with the rest, to vegetate.
While I've still got my faculties to boast about
Can I make it clear now, how I want to go out
If I reach that pearly gate, at my final toll
I hope that he'll consider me, a timeless soul
I smile through faded eyes, remembering my prime
But you, me, or no man, can cheat the tides of time . . .
Maura T Bye

Recollections
The eager plough lies rusty now,
The well is long since dry,
The oaken door of the old corn store
Hangs open to the sky.

No need to reap the long eared wheat
The fields in slumber lie,
No need to gaze on Nature's ways
With anxious watchful eye.

Yet memory remains to me
Despite the year's decline,
Of boyhood days, of breathless days,
Of elms I used to climb.

Of village school, of trout ringed pool,
Of woodland's welcome shade,
Of rich red earth hard worked and worth
The sweat my father gave.

Brown limbed and burned by summer sun
My place was at his side,
As in my turn I sought to learn
Beneath those patient eyes.

And then alone I steered this land,
I learnt its moods and ways,
I knew it in its gentleness
And wild tempestuous days.

And though I stand grey bearded now
Beside an idle rustling plough,
And though the wind has left the mill
I know this land is breathing still.
Gerry Knight

The Valiant Few
In 1940 the skies over England were blue
That summer, when the valiant few
With spitfires and Hurricane
Took to the skies.
To guard our shores, the future looked dark
The German invasion, seemed so near at hand
To threaten the peace, of this beautiful land.
With 'We'll meet again.'
And that 'Lovely weekend.'
To sweethearts and wives
With tear-filled eyes, they waved their good-byes,
Those valiant boys, and made for the skies
Now forty years on, the spitfires are gone.

The young men, so bold, now have grown old,
And the Nightingale, still sings in the park
The Germans we managed to keep at bay
Now we trade with every day.
For England they came
And they'd do it again
So let's not forget as the years hurry by
When in summer you look up to the sky
And give thanks to God,
For the valiant few
Who saved this land, when the skies were blue
For that freedom cost, so many young lives
Who never came back
To loved ones and wives.
Irene G Corbett

The Budget

Petrol up thirteen pence a gallon!
November ninety three, the Budget's here again,
It's pay more for your cigarettes, or a trip abroad by plane;
Where's the money coming from? Incomes still the same.
The tax man said, 'Seventeen pence extra, on every pound,
                                    you'll pay on your fuel bill.'
Then came a little sugar, to coat this bitter pill,
'A rebate for all pensioners,' that really was a laugh,
Just a ruse to hide the fact, they'll pay the other half.

Car tax is going up and house insurance too,
Where's the money coming from? No windfall from the blue.
Do you smoke a cigarette or two, and go to work by car, on roads
                                    where tolls are due?
Each week, you're bound to feel the pinch, at least nine
                                    pounds or so.
Christmas time is coming up; presents will be few.
If your bank account, can stand the strain, maybe you'll
                                    scrape through.

What about the folk at home, who haven't got a job?
What about the old folk, who sit by a cold hob?
For them, it's less of this, and less of that,
                              shop prices are so dear;
What sort of Christmas will be theirs?
                              Not very bright I fear.
No comfort, for the homeless; young and old, their outlook
                                        stark and drear.
For them; no glad new tidings, in this coming Budget Year!
Irene Tonks

Love is

The heart burns with sincere devotion,
Eyes give away truest emotions,
Bodies touching in loving embraces,
Love is born in many places.

The everlasting experience lingers,
The bodies mind tingles
Lips melting in passion,
Love is born in many a fashion.

Soft caresses searching,
Bodies flesh yearning,
Secret places awaken,
Love is born to be taken.

The bodies hungers meet,
And two people seek
Cupid has awoken mans love for woman,
Love is born never to be forgotten.
Tina Kemp

A Missing Soldier

Sat on a bar stool, her hand round a bottle
A packet of cigarettes close by her hand,
Dressed in a fashion that dates from the forties
Our kids of today would not understand.

Her hair is tied back with a black satin ribbon
Silvery grey where her brown curls once grew
Her face is so aged with wrinkles and sadness
Watching the door for her love to walk through.

Her heart is a book that takes plenty of reading
With traces of tear drops that stain every page.
The photo she carries it torn at the edges,
Pale is the print as it's fading with age.

She's bearing the scars of the wartime and after
She's bearing the heartache of what had to be
She sits there, still waiting alone for her soldier
Her soldiers not coming, his spirit roams free.
S A Crowley

Little Man

Little man, why do you drive a big car?
It isn't as though you travel very far,
Stuck in the traffic,
Stuck in a queue,
Burning up oil,
Leaded petrol too,
Harder to park,
More coveted to steal,
Do you really think,
That you've such a good deal?
Little man why do you drive a big car?
It isn't as though you travel very far.
Valerie Taylor

131

Old Steam

An old steam train
Puffing away its song
Rivet steel round heat
On the old rails it's gone,
The red faced stoker
Shovels in embedded spade
And the driver measures the steam
And how many miles he'd made.

And it's old steam, old train
I can remember that far back
In my mind
The trains are still living
As I walk along this old track
And its old steam, old train
Past old stations and signal box
In my mind
I see the porter at the station
As the next old train, stops by.

An old steam train
And a railway that's been
Rusty old rails meet
Under brick arches
Long and dim
The small boys taking engine numbers
As the big engine
Goes underneath
On its way to a destination
Leaving its memories in peace.

An old steam train
In an old steam yard
Looking lost and rusty now
Not like when it was the western star

You see the trains on picture postcards
When we knew all their names
Now waiting for resurrection
By the old steam fans.
Stuart Terry Munro

Inherited Treasures
I often wonder what will become
Of my beloved treasures when I've gone
To Great Aunt Em's teaset and the moustache cup
And the loudly ticking marble clock.

The cup given to father from World War One,
The blue Worcester bowl from my husband's home
My Victorian plate dated 1 - 8 - 9 - 7
When hopefully I have gone to heaven.

My mother's rings, my husband's watch
His bookcase and the spoons that match
Piano and organ that gave us such pleasure
When we were happy and living together.

There's scarce a home in the whole of the land
That hasn't a treasure from a departed hand
Can I therefore make this plea?
'Treat them gently, they were loved by me!'
Vera F Coaton

Railways of My Youth
Those steam trains of yesterday that went into decline
By Beeching act and other means, now as the coal mine
Are kept in smaller enclaves by a preservation few
Of dedicated people, enjoying what they do,
Trains that puffed and moved along unlike the modern diesel kind
That have no romance anywhere and are still quite hard to find

With railways shrinking year by year and privatised as well
No public transport mode it seems commuters lives are hell.
With rising fares, lower standards, fewer train to serve their needs
More and more have clogged highways in the car capsules we breed
And those juggernauts like lorries have also helped the decline
Of a most previous asset, the good old railway line,
In the days of yore every hamlet had a halt
Cuttings, bridges and viaducts the clickery clack and the jolt
The smell of smoke and steam through towns and countryside
All across this land linking people nation-wide.
Railway children were we all playing by some line
On bridges smoke and steam, swirling around us we thought fine
Watching the signals from signal boxes by railway men of old
Other chaps on maintenance, porters with badges gold,
Carrying cases issuing tickets keeping stations smart and clean
In every hamlet, village and township, now just a memory it seems
In the name of what's called progress into history gone
Museums the only link now left and where amateurs still throng.
Among the rolling stock lines and stations, coal wood and steam
Doing their preservation hobby, make old engines really gleam
A delight for our descendants to enjoy in some small way
The railways of our yesteryear we older folks enjoyed each day
                                                    of youth.

Philip Temperton

Dousing the Candle
Our captains name was Randle
On the S S Devon Caprice
And we called the mate Candle
Because he came from Greece.

We tidied up the ship
As we sailed across the bay
I shall remember this trip
When I am old and grey.

We were not very smart
You would call us a motley crew
But right from the start
We all knew what to do.

One day the skipper said to the mate
'It's time you had a shave
Your uniform is in a hell of a state
Have you just crawled out of a grave.'

The mate called the skipper a ruddy snob
And kicked a bucket over the side
He said 'I am here to do my job
You are only here for the ride.'

Then the skipper he let rip
As he stood by the after hatch
At Plymouth port you will leave the ship
That's how candle met his match.
Roy Welch

Blackpool Revisited
No passports or visa, door to door in an hour
To the jewel of the west coast, well known for its tower.
As I stroll down the prom, my mind is cast
Back to vacations in Blackpool, long ago in the past.
A toddler on the beach, complete with bucket and spade
Splashing through shallow breakers enjoying a wade.
Young teenagers, in the dark early days of war
Rationing and restrictions our pleasure did mar,
Landlady saying, I have managed to beg,
Some black market bacon to go with your dried egg.
Around the winter gardens, in the arms of a holiday romance.
Flirtatious fumblings in the blackout after the dance,
Low flying RAF planes, skimming the skies
Fat ladies on saucy postcards, saying 'Wish you were here.'

A few years on but seemed much later
For a family, Blackpool now had to cater,
Three small boys my wife and a folding pram
To the boating pool at Bispharm, on the upper deck of a tram.
Asleep in a deckchair oblivious to everything
Children catch small crabs, with a short piece of string,
Three small boys, my wife and I,
In a rain swept shelter, playing *I spy*.
It rained then in inches, lest we forget
Now it's in millimetres, but still just as wet,
No high rise hotels, paella, fish soup or squid
But revisiting Blackpool has saved a few quid,
A Squires Gate chalet, compact and neat
With tea maker, coloured telly and of course en suite.
Indeed this became a holiday unique
For the blessed sun shone, every day of the week.
Raymond Winston Aspden

Away From Home
When children grow and leave the home,
A mother often feels alone.
Her children often fill her dreams,
No longer there to share their schemes.
Her thoughts are all for days gone past,
Wishing they'd not flown so fast.
Perhaps tomorrow there'll be a letter?
Or a phone call, that's even better!
Their life and future is theirs alone,
Especially now they're not at home,
Where mum could keep them in her care,
Worries not for them to bear.
For all the children away from home,
Have some thought for mum - alone!
Kathleen Mileham

136

Day Dreams
Yesterday is gone,
Tomorrow is a dream.
Today is what we live for
No matter what it brings.
So treasure yesterday memories
And keep them locked away
Don't worry for tomorrow
For it will come and go
Today is what's important
So take it as it comes
And when it ends and it's time
To sleep
Tomorrow will be today.
R Read

The Days are Cold and Lonely
The days are cold and lonely
The nights are seldom warm,
Love lies dead and long forgotten,
There's nothing left to mourn.

The days are cold and lonely
There's a weight upon my heart.
The hours are long and endless,
It's forever we're apart.

The days are cold and lonely,
The dark is oft my friend
To drown in depths of sorrow
With silence at the end.

The days are cold and lonely
Wrapped in deep despair
To think and now forever
That you never more will care.
Eve Twyman

137

An Ode to Clive

There once was a gang of odd jobbers,
Led by a chargehand called Clive,
Resplendent in glo-brighter clobber,
They were the fastest broom pushers alive.

They called themselves proudly the 'A' team,
No job was too big or too tough,
They left their streets tidy and so clean,
For their foreman they could not do enough.

Now our Clive is a man just and fair,
Protecting his men from the weather,
He sends his men here and sometimes over there,
Saying 'I love it when a plan comes together.'

But Clive has just one small weakness,
And that's Greenie, the thorn in his side,
One look at his face and Clive's helpless,
His laughter he just cannot hide.

Never mind Clive, the gang's right behind you,
Their loyalty is a joy to behold,
But is their desire to please too good to be true?
Clive, don't worry, or too soon you'll be old.

Take it easy, forget the sweet wrappers,
And the fag ends that stick to the floor,
Here comes Colin saying 'Don't worry, just trust me,'
Let's face it, what man could want more?
C E Green

Counting our Blessings

The stresses and strains of everyday life,
The news ever bad, full of wars and strife.
The hatred, the violence, the greed and disease,
Millions are starving - no water, no seeds.

138

Yet here in this country - we moan and we groan,
We have TV and video's, hi fi and phones,
Complain when we're hungry, got to hop in the car,
To refill our cupboards - from our local Spar!

Perhaps we should take the time to imagine -
Just what it is like with no flesh on our limbs.
And to really know hunger - with all of the pain -
To see our own children - dying and lame.

So rather than moan, and forever complain,
Rejoice in your family and treasure each day.
When your child runs to you for tender caressing -
You've no greater reason - for counting your blessings.
J Rulton

People

People are funny creatures
They shout and moan and scream
It's not enough you see them all day
But you see them at night when you dream.

People are funny creatures
Some even make you cry
There's nothing like the feeling you get
When one of them tells you a lie.

People are funny creatures
Some even make you laugh
There's nothing like the laughter you get
When you see them all pink in the bath.

People are funny creatures
Some even think they can sing
Have you ever heard their voices
They make your earholes ring.

People are funny creatures
God made them so I'm told
It's alright for the first few years
But then they get quite old.

People are funny creatures
I think I'll get one for a pet
I understand that some can swim
So I wouldn't mind getting it wet.

People are funny creatures
My dad said I'm one too
I didn't think that I was one
I only thought they were you.
Jacqueline Smith

Friendship

'Tis was a November day,
A good friendship came our way,
Good friendships don't grow on trees,
It takes trust and loyalty.

In this world of deceit and lust,
It's good to have friends that you trust,
Their hearts and ours beat as one,
With this friendship that's begun.

Jealousy, lies are far from mind,
With two great people that are so kind.
They give you love - that's treasured so much,
A kind of love you just can't touch.

The warmth you feel when they're near,
Means your friendship is so dear.
There's tears you wish - you could kiss away,
Only love - in them to stay.

When times are hard and smiles are few,
Just remember what (You must do)
Help them - cry with them - love them - show them you care,
Say to them you're always be there.

The months go by and turn to years,
Shared their love and shared their tears.
Friends of ours, they'll always be,
A part of us - our family.
R A Matthews

Life is Great
When morning breaks and the sun peeps thro'
The day has dawned and I'm glad it's true,
That life is great and we all renew -
Friendships lost - partners failed -
Safe in the knowledge our ships have sailed.

The day it rains, it's pleasant too -
Because God's plan - for earth - and me - and you -
Brings us closer together - in bonds of love -
In knowing that raindrops come from Him above.

Spring has its blessings, autumn too,
Flowers abound and bird song breaks thro
They're not afraid to look to the sky -
Animals creep along the ground -
And listen for a familiar sound
It could be you or I they greet
For to them - life is sweet.

All the good things of life are free -
If only we stop - and bend a knee -
A friendly smile, a pat on the head,
An extended hand, a good wish from a friend,
Many more too if only we cared -
To listen and love and announce
Life is great.
                                                    Margaret Kirkham

We Came

We came upon this earth
You and me
All those years ago
But where are we now?
Thee and thou
Now that we have bled
This earth that we tread,
It's to late to go back
To try another track,
We had our chance
But we did not enhance
This earth that we live on today.
Albert Swainson

Life

I love the morning
I wake with the dawning
So very quiet. No sound.
The dew still on the ground.
I sit, listen and wait.
In stillness i meditate.
Such joy now in life.
When there is no strife.
Where only love grows
In many ways, it shows.
How much joy we bring.
Which makes all hearts sing.
For all blessings received.
For all life has weaved.
Each year has seen change
Sometimes so very strange.
And we do not understand
Only divine spirit has planned

We can only live each day,
Enjoy life fully and pray
That we have truly cared.
Loved all and shared.
This and every day.
There is no other way.
Jan Wood

When I Grow Up . . .
I always said I'm different from you
I know what I want and I'll get it too.
Thought of myself, hard, clever and knowing.
When I grow up, I'll do it this way,
When I grow up, I'll know where I'm going.
I'll have me a man, a house and some money.
My folks they laughed, what was so funny!
Little did I know, they'd lived longer than me,
They saw the future, they'd paid the fee.

I said no children, just fun, this is my life.
I'll work little, play hard, I'll be no ones wife.
Just to travel and dance. I'd love just a few and
When I get bored, I'll read, take a pew.
My friends will surround me, we'll laugh and we'll laugh,
Great wit will confound me, I'll do things not by half.
Age could not touch my existence so full
Incessant youth, would only befall.

I had the fun, sand and sea, did the jobs
One, two and three,
Escaped is the man, my friends escaped me,
Single mothers my title, I suppose I've grown wise,
Now I'm the one giving advice,
I'm thirty six now, not old some may say
But I'm still waiting for 'every dog has his day.'
Susan Purkiss

Yesteryear
Days of youth that I recall
Fishing in a shallow pool
Wading in amongst the mud
Strolling through the bluebell wood,
Rolling down rough bank of grass
Careful round the narrow pass
Games we played on winter days
Snow covered hills and home-made sleighs.
Fivestones played with stones so bright,
Fireworks and guys on bonfire night,
These are the things that I recall
Happy days for one and all.
Julia Yardley

Here to Eternity
There's all sorts of things that we look at
And all sorts of things that we see,
There's all sorts of things we venture to do,
From here to eternity.
There's all sorts of different people
In all walks of life you will agree,
They are really just ordinary people
Just the same as you and me.
Some maybe a little bit richer
There's different colours and creed,
But there comes a time in everyone's life,
When we all have our hours of need.
Joan Sadler

Misunderstanding
Children should not have to suffer
at the hands of ignorance
these tiny little mortals
should be given a better chance
deprived they may be of affection
deprived of the love they may seek.

Those guilty don't blame or condemn them
for their soles are not strong they are weak
so before we can teach all our children
dear Lord why not teach us all first
that the love which we find hard to handle
fill our soles with that love till we burst.
Susan Day

Poem of Departure
I'm not going to run
through the park any more,
staring at the stars at night, drunk
in the summer of sensitive friends
past the fairground, laughing
at girls and acting so mad and wild
or walk along the park by the pond
          because I'm dreaming
          of going away.

I'm not going to walk
along the High Street
past cafes, chip shops and bookshops
any more. A year and a half
has been quite enough. I'm dreaming
of the country. I shall walk
through the night with my lover
in some psychiatric hospital,
fairground or home
          far away.

Events have gone around
and around and around and around
in my life. Things turn full circle.
The past relives itself in my reeling
mind full of galaxies and quasars
and all night cafes near Trafalgar
Square. Nelson's column is toppling,
and I will emigrate to the vaster,
more natural fountain of the sea
          where midnight lovers bathe.
Trains are like snakes
In the vast night
And I shall love and laugh over
My initiation rite.
Peter Mackie

Rage and Rebellion

I was chucked out of school, below normal.
Exams were a problem to me.
I could not remember what king or queen
Reigned and as for Geography,
Rivers and mountains were coloured blue and
Green, on a small map of the world.
But I could not draw, so that my
Coastline was crinkled, as though it has been curled.
The voice of the teacher, in front of the class
Shrieked forth with a threatening shout
'Do you call that Wales lad I wonder why,
You bothered to pencil it out?'
And as for maths I could not add up,
Divide or take away
Peculiar problems destorted my mind,
So a truant I became each day
Now you will agree a child must eat,
But how can he buy without money.

146

So a thief I became, and grabbed
What I could, till a bobby cried
'Sonny
Come along with me' you know
The
Rest of the tale and the awful truth
Is, I became a wilful
Truant
A rebellious wandering youth.
Edith Ray

The Saga of Radio Ron
This is the saga of *Radio Ron*
nobody missed him until he had gone.
He first started working for BOAC
learning the aeroplanes drinking the tea.

Starting with *Argies* he's worked on them all
obviously dropping an occasional ball!
Britannia's and *Comets*, *Connies* and *Strats*,
his wisecracks and puns drove his mates to the Lats!

Then one day he just didn't turn up
so somebody else had to drink from his cup.
An *attack of the heart* so the doctor did say,
Nothing much else would have kept him away.

Off to St George's on April the first
The agony of waiting was by far the worst.
A coronary by-pass was then carried out
and soon out bed he was limping about.

Several weeks later and feeling much better
the time has arrived to continue this letter.
To thank all of you for all your good wishes,
to thoughts of retirement and doing the dishes.

To him there's a bonus for working on planes
Much more variation than most jobs can claim.
Then there's the fellows that he's working with,
quite a few things that he's likely to miss.

But there comes a time in every man's life
to sit by the fire and pester the wife!
To work in the garden, go fishing for trout,
So *cheerio* friends, it's time to get out.
Ronald C Houghton

Men!

What is a man I dare to ask?
Such a formidable task
Entering the *lion's* den
Probing into minds of men.

Gentle, nice and calm of mind
While others blast at all mankind.
Those with bloated ego's think
That any girl who cares to shrink
From their advances is a bore -
Ignore her - then will meet no more.

Some will seek a pretty girl
With shining eyes and hair a-curl
But later on might find her slow -
'Her IQ's not that good you know!'
An advantageous streak for some
Who like to overlord the dumb.

Men are only grown-up boys
Who play with trains and other toys.
Like rough games and drinking beer
Singing so their friends might hear
Their *lovely* voices - loud and clear.

Then will slump into a seat
To air opinions - *such* a treat.
A *show-off* is the worst for me
Puffed up with pride for all to see.

So, what *is* a man, again I plead
As one for years who's tried to read
Their clockwork minds, which sometimes *tick*
But who often make me *sick*!
K M Blackwood

Still Friends
With confident air
With auburn hair
Friends from the start
Sincere at heart
Freckled of face, I'll never erase
Complexion clean, peaches and cream
Welsh she spoke and hand in hand
A special bond
Had a ball, sharing all
Tidy and neat, the world to meet
Edith Bach
Navy blue and white tie just right
Polished shoes and black stockinged legs
A special time, our hearts entwine
Step out together, taking care
Having words, there we were
Spending youth, smiles and tears
Those two years
On the Mull, never dull
Dear to my heart, Edith Bach
As chalk and cheese, we tried to please
Told me off, never strayed from womanly ways
Keep in touch, remembering when
You were a Wren
My other half, Edith Bach.
Constance Moseley

The Autumn of Life

Life used to be so good,
A pleasure to awake!
Life used to be so good,
So good for heavens sake,
Life used to be a joy to live,
With children on my knee
Life used to be so very good
When you were here with me!

But now the years have passed
Just like a whistling train,
And I'm left all alone in life
All alone in pain,
Oh how I miss your laughter and the love
we held so dear!
When children depended most on us
to dispel their every fear.

Now I'm left alone with pain each and
every night
It gets worse and worse, too bad for me to fight,
And as I look across the room, my eyes grow
oh so dim!
A moonbeam flickers in the night, and the life
goes out within!
Then as my spirit leaves; there comes another
dawn,
And somewhere across this great big world
another child is born.
Michael David Sparkes

Misguided Youth

Lost in a tunnel of deepest despair
deluded, discouraged, unanswered prayer
Cries of anguish in a forgotten world
In space motionless hopelessly hurled

150

What reason, what purpose was I ever made?
Why was life given, what price is paid?
Where is the God we cannot see?
How can God care for me?

This world of selfish driving nation
Reckless living, no loyalty or devotion
How cruel we treat at one another
Jealous hatred for sister or brother

If we are made like him above
How can God be a God of love?
Look at the suffering, the senseless injustice
The wicked prosper, the righteous flourish

The innocent lie in graves with no names
Men with power, play at war games
Pride rules governments in high places
Fear runs riot, I'm all races

Military men parade with relicts of destruction
Cold blank faces wait melancholy for instruction
Pompous proper gramda to show feats of strength
Competitions expeditions of heights and length
A little fish in a great big sea
How can anybody consider me?
Iris Grice

Nige's Poem
I lie in my bedroom,
Crashed out on my bed,
I look at my walls
As I listen to Ned's.

My walls are covered,
From ceiling to floor,
With posters of Carter,
Who I just adore.

The next thing I know,
I'm next to Fruitbat,
And Jimbob is dancing
With Holly, my cat!

We talked and we laughed,
And we started to sing,
But who should arrive?
The Sultans of Ping!

The lead singer thinks
That he's it,
He even called me
A permissive little shit!

Then I *blinked*,
I was back in my room,
Looked out of the window
And stared at the moon.

I must've been dreaming,
No one was there,
Except for Holly,
Asleep on the chair.
Bow Harrison

Alone
Alone, in a room
with a book full of friends,
All alone on my own,
I wait for the end.
On my own, I am alone,
It is not difficult to comprehend
Why I cry out for joy
When I think of the end.
James L Taylor

The Beast Within the Human Mask
This dark force has no face
But one design
To still the beating heart
And conquer time,
No sheltering path
Forever the servant to its
Own awesome wrath
A merciless rage
Knowing only to forsake
No crown of divinity.
As the given breath it takes
From early growth it does arise
To form and bear the same disguise,
The mask of death
And blood desire
To shroud the genius
Torments within the howling
Sea of Fire.

Michael J Ryan

Friendship
When you are despondent,
When you're feeling blue,
When it seems the whole wide world
is ganging up on you -
Is there someone, somewhere
Not too far away
One you can rely on to brighten
Up your day
Someone you can talk to - and
don't have to pretend?
Then you must count your blessings,
For you have got a friend.

Vera N Mason

153

Retired

At seventy eight I like
my dinner on my plate
Turkey and greens, jelly and
cream with a glass of water
Is a wonderful meal

What's for tea? Marmalade you see
No cake for me or silly cream
I have got to live for twenty five pence
It won't be long
How quickly time has gone
Never mind I am still alive
Content, a smile.
Florence Clara Garner

I Do Care - Honest!

You know it's a *sin* to worry . . . yet worry we often do
Perhaps I'm only talking about me, and not of course of you!
I don't care what others think - is what I always say . . .
And yet I know I will be hurt by someone else today.

A thickish skin is what I possess, I keep my feelings hid!
Crying's a thing, I ain't done since I was a little kid.
Singing out loud . . . at work or play . . . is summat I always do
I tend to find that the melody just seems to help me through!

But you know there are people, who resent it when you're glad
They seem to walk round all day, with a face that looks so sad
Singing just comes so naturally - keeps on bubbling out of me
Sometimes I whistle, just as bad, that also makes some folk mad!

Now I'm not a mind-reader . . . but I do really care
I am always willing a burden to share . . .
But I can't tell . . . if folks don't tell me
So I just keep singing away merrily.

A few poor mortals carry spite as they go
What brought it on, I never shall know!
Perhaps they're unhappy with the life that they live
Because a smile or a kind word - they just never give!

I mustn't judge - for you can't tell a book by its cover
They might have been happy, until spurned by a lover . . .
Or tortured as children - or hounded in youth
One day, perhaps, I might find the truth!

I call on you people . . .let's make a deal
Don't nag at me . . . say how you feel . . .
If I knew your feelings, I'd know how to act . . .
Because I do really care, I do, that's a fact!
Steve Clarke

My Job

A childminder is my job,
It's not that easy to earn a bob,
Toys over here, toys over there,
For all our friends to come and share,
My child could shout and scream all day long,
At end of day I'm glad she's gone,
We sit and play and learn too,
Then she cries, she having a poo,
I clean her up and change her bum,
Let us go and have some fun,
Get on her coat she screams with glee,
It's great going out you see,
Go to the shops, and on the swings,
It's quite easy to do all these things,
She goes for a sleep. I'd take a peep,
I wonder if she's counting sheep,
I'm having a rest with an hour to spare,
So leave me alone if you care,

Then it's time for tea, let's eat,
Oh, I do feel quite beat,
Baby's mum comes at last,
How the day seems to go quite fast,
Cleaning, tidying all those toys
Oh my, what a noise,
Take a bath wash my hair,
Now I don't seem to really care
Watch TV and have some fun,
That's all that needs to be done.
Christine Kowalkowski

The Rocking Horse

I live in the attic,
At the top of the house.
My only companion
A little grey mouse.
The days are long,
The nights so cold.
I have plenty of time,
For memories to unfold.
I see all the children
There faces aglow,
As they climbed on my back,
I would rock too and fro,
Off we would gallop
to far away places,
Faster, faster was the cry,
From their smiling faces.
Tea is ready, someone would shout.
Then all the children,
Just ran out.
I'm not dreaming now
As I hear a voice say.
Bring down the rocking house.
My grandson's coming to stay.
Margaret Trodd

Wedding Day
On our wedding day, the sun shines bright,
Our love is plain to see,
As we stand together, hands entwined,
Our future's meant to be.

We repeat the words as our eyes meet,
And we both have this feeling,
We pledge our love until we die,
Our thoughts and minds are reeling.

Suddenly, we are man and wife,
Together we are bound,
We go outside into the sun,
A new life we have found.

Our wedding day has been a dream,
It's goodbye to the past,
We've laughed and loved and cried alot,
But the future's ours at last.
Susan Lanham-Cook

Lovers or Friends?
Somewhere in the night time sky
There is a star where you and I could be together,
Where we won't mind the weather
But mind whether we would find the peace of mind we need,
The love on which we'd feed upon
To make up for the years we starved inside,
When we held our breath, then sighed,
And then sat alone and cried.

But the love that's now and real
Is so close that you can feel the heat
That makes the special bond complete.
And the dreams of what could still be true
Can be shared in a place that's just for two
And then in the end,
As lovers or friends,
There will be no more need to pretend.
Steve J Case

Conversation

I'm old, grey and just living from
Day to day.
What's that you muttered?
I'm so very deaf
I didn't hear a word you uttered.
But . . . I can see-hear, and converse
If these small things you will do first.

Please, look at me, it's your lips I want to see.
Move them when you talk.
I'll read them, as taught.
Stand, or sit, facing the light.
Yes. That's right.
Please don't shout.
My hearing aid will vibrate at any loud
Noise you make.

Now let us converse.
Will you start first?
I'll read your lips, you'll hear words from mine.
That's right. That's just fine.
Now I can see-hear.
Thank you.
My dear.
Linda Clear

Is it Only a Day?
(In memory of our son Gordon Daniel born 4.10.1976 died
24.11.1993, aged 17)

Is it only a day
Since we read your letter
With dad's birthday cards?

Is it only a week
Since we walked round the lake
In the rain?
Had tea and cake and didn't mention
The chocolate shop.

Is it only a year
Since you and dad walked with me
My first unsteady steps
After illness?

Only seventeen years
Since they gave you oxygen
To help you live
When you came half-strangled
Into this world.

Now machines and tubes
Monitor life;
Easing your breath
Till death.
Ruth Daniel

Life Class

Plump stillness enfolded in pose, pale planes
elusive in the shadowed half light
which cushions the sharper debits
and erosions. The spine's sensual undulation
draws down to rounded delight
in a leading, eliding rhythm of line and mind.
Flow, fall and fierce awareness harmonise
with her unsparing figure.

Perspective in parts is unconvincing
and tricks of the light are sometimes subtly caught, sometimes
botched.
You can be pleased with that angle
which echoes a faithful curve
but there's a corner where the paper thinned
in vain pursuit of a nuance
which never really worked, effort past ability.

Starting again, it might be better, certainly different
but this is the being you've painfully fashioned.
Charles Kaye

Untitled

If all the world was mine to give
I'd give it all to you.
But the world is not mine to give,
So my love will have to do.
If I held the heavens in my hands
I'd lay them at your feet,
All the stars would be your crown
The moon would be your seat.
None of these things can I do
For the one that I adore.
So all that I can offer
Is to love you more and more.
D J Watkins

Four Minutes to Sunrise

The room is still, I am ready,
The RSM is steady, I am guilty,
In darkness lies my life,
The last few morsels to savour,
A banquet to the last, my saviour,
Four minutes to sunrise,
Let no man grieve, I must die.

Is all this just for me?
Me! Private, in my entirety,
On my way to eternity.
I look into these eyes,
I see no warmth or justice,
Three minutes to sunrise,
May God forgive you, I must die.

Two years, I did as I was bid,
In my private hell-holed sanity,
Twice shell-holed lunacy,
They dragged me back to reality,
And in those eyes I see my cruelty,
Two minutes to sunrise,
Oh Lord forgive me, I must die.

Two years, you'll soon be rid,
For my running scared, you give mortality,
And the huns lead, taught morality,
To the boys, who weren't men,
And in those schoolroom eyes, fatality,
One minute to sunrise,
Lord don't let me see them when I die.

And the sun finished my breakfast,
devoured greedily my life to the last,
Lord forgive me, please take my as I die.
George Luke

161